WAKE TECHNICAL COMMUNITY COLLEGE LIBRARY
9101 FAYETTEVILLE ROAD
RALEIGH, NORTH CAROLINA 27603

Consequential Learning

Consequential Learning

A Public Approach To Better Schools

Jack Shelton

NewSouth Books
Montgomery

NewSouth Books
P.O. Box 1588
Montgomery, AL 36102

Copyright © 2005 by Jack Shelton
All rights reserved under International and Pan-American Copyright Conventions. Published in the United States by NewSouth Books, a division of NewSouth, Inc., Montgomery, Alabama.

Library of Congress Cataloging-in-Publication Data

Shelton, Jack.
Consequential learning : a public approach to better schools / Jack Shelton.
p. cm.
Includes bibliographical references.
ISBN 1-58838-185-4 (hardcover) — ISBN 1-58838-186-2 (pbk.)
1. School improvement programs—United States. 2. Community and school—United States. 3. Rural education—Alabama. I. Title.
LB2822.82.S44 2005
371.2'00973—dc22
2005008099

Printed in the United States of America

IN MEMORY OF
PATTI LOGAN AND LISA ANDERSON CHALMERS
GOOD TEACHERS, AND GOOD FRIENDS

Contents

Foreword / 9

Preface / 13

Introduction / 21

Section 1:
  The Inspiration for Consequential Learning / 28

Section 2:
  Consequential Learning Principles / 59

Section 3:
  Consequential Learning in Action / 79

Section 4:
  Consequential Learning Issues / 110

Conclusion:
  How Public is Public Education? / 143

Notes / 148

Bibliography / 151

Foreword

David Mathews

Most books about education are implicitly books about politics. This one certainly is. *Consequential Learning* is about democratic politics, in which citizens derive their just power from what they make through collective decisions and actions. It is also about what my friend Robert McClintock at Columbia University calls "a place for study in a world of instruction." The two are related. Learning is a quintessential democratic practice. Citizens must be capable of learning what has to be done to solve common problems because in a democracy we don't allow any coercive authority to tell us what to do. Collective or civic learning ensures freedom.

I hope teachers and administrators will read what Jack Shelton has to say, but this is primarily a book for citizens. The book is about education, and education is about more than schooling. Education is accessible to people; they can all have some hand in it. Americans aren't so sure about schooling because it seems to be a professional domain. Jack describes how the educational work of citizens can complement and reinforce schools. The message for overburdened, hardworking teachers and administrators is to seek out the natural allies in communities. They aren't alone in the larger work of education.

The community is the natural setting for *Consequential Learning*. Jack remembers what is often forgotten these days: schools are more than marketplaces selling information to customers. They are community-maintaining institutions. That is especially so in small, rural communities. If the school closes, the community usually dies. Jack is well-known around the country for what he has to say about rural education. He explains why closing small schools may actually cost more than it saves. A closing affects the overall economy, not just a school board's budget. When a school closes, the community loses a big chunk of the social capital that fuels growth, as economists have shown. Jack argues that schools can actually be engines for economic development in hard-pressed communities. Creative, entrepreneurial people have transformed areas like northwest Arkansas. Jack gives examples of schools that have fostered the same spirit of enterprise. Certainly the quality of community life is an asset in attracting new industry, and there again Jack cites what schools have done.

I got to know Jack when he was the United Methodist campus minister at the University of Alabama. He took his students to small Alabama communities where they worked with local citizens on educational, agricultural, health, and other projects. His work speaks to today's concern about the current college generation's understanding of citizenship. Jack's students have been more than individuals providing services; they have learned what it means to be members of a community. I thought he was one of the best professors of applied democracy in the country; you'll see why when he describes the Program for Rural Services and Research and its predecessor, the Student

Coalition for Community and Health. The coalition fit well with the University of Alabama's efforts to develop a College of Community Health Sciences that would draw from all its schools to combat the appalling lack of health care in a rural state. These student programs contributed significantly to the formation of the PACERS Cooperative, which I hope will become an enduring civic structure combining democracy and public education.

The campus projects took on some of the major problems we are now confronting in public education, such as the citizenry's declining sense of ownership of the schools, reflected in the perception that "these aren't our schools." When ownership declines, so does a sense of collective responsibility. PACERS has fought this trend; the coalition sponsored projects in which citizens made things through their collective efforts and schools drew on these products of public work to enrich their curriculum. This work helped restore a sense of community ownership and responsibility. People are more inclined to take responsibility when their own handiwork is involved. My favorite examples are the aquaculture projects. In the small Alabama town of Florala, community members proudly provided a fishery that became a living laboratory for the sciences. In Loachapoka, citizens did the same thing when they joined forces to build a greenhouse for their school.

If your instincts tell you that a place teaches, you will find yourself in good company. The ability of a citizenry to make local settings available for instructional purposes is a demonstration of what "just folks" can do. Not everyone can teach algebra, but everyone can contribute to the education of young people. Everything from a creek running through town to the local newspapers have been used to create living laboratories.

Education is more than test scores, textbooks, and professional expertise. All of these have their place. But education is as much an enterprise of the soul as it is of the mind. And Jack Shelton reminds us of that on every page.

A native of Clarke County, Alabama, David Mathews is president of the Kettering Foundation. He previously served as president of the University of Alabama and as secretary of the U.S. Department of Health, Education, and Welfare.

Preface

Over a span of thirty years, it has been my good fortune to be associated with young persons engaged in a variety of challenging programs through which they developed personally and academically and produced results that have made their places better. I have written this book in response to their good work and that of the adults who supported them. It is my purpose, even obligation, to delineate the implications of their efforts and to share and apply their insights which are relevant to the ongoing tasks of improving schools and communities, and preparing young people to be good citizens in a democratic society and effective participants in the economy.

It is my hope that this book will help bring together community members, potential school resource persons—especially those with professional expertise—policy makers, funders, and educators to work together to link learning to place and to reach the attainable goals set forward under the rubric of Consequential Learning. I especially look forward to the ongoing efforts of those individuals and organizations that are partners in PACERS from which many of the programs and approaches of

Consequential Learning have been derived and will continue to be implemented. It is my deepest desire that this book will help further the work of that association.

It was inevitable in writing this book and reflecting on the experiences central to it that I made comparisons with my own education. In an interview included in Sara Day Hatton's *Teaching by Heart: The Foxfire Interviews*, I answered her question about my most memorable learning experience in school by citing my sixth grade assignment to write play to be performed in front of my classmates, our parents, and invited guests from the community. It was the only time—as far as memory serves—in my formal education that I was asked to use academic tools to create a tangible, public outcome. The responsibility was greater than that for any test, but the response was more affirming and gave a new relevance to my school work. The experiences of students involved in programs described in this book are not unlike my own sixth grade venture, but they go far beyond what I has the chance to do. Of course I wish that I had had similar opportunities, but, more importantly, I believe they can and should be available routinely for all our kids. The experiences on which this book is based have raised deep concerns about schooling and have confirmed approaches that have demonstrated considerable promise.

In my observations, the passive—and by implication insufficiently democratic—nature of education, the decontextualization of curriculum, and the growing divide between schools and their publics are among the disquieting matters that have routinely surfaced. On the positive side, it is clear that linking learning to place provides powerful incentives for students and teachers. Young persons are ready to do good work and to be challenged as learners and as members of communities. Many adults—educators, community members, and professional resource persons—are prepared to help them. I have become convinced that students want to produce public outcomes as a part of their schooling. They want to make a difference. They want and need the affirmation and support of their communities—which I believe they are prepared to give. In fact communities are ready to take greater roles in schools and in the educating of young people.

Most of the work underpinning this book was done in ethnically and economically diverse rural Alabama schools that more often than not are underresourced and that have a very high proportion of students living in poverty. However, the successes of students and teachers testify to their abilities and commitment and to the applicability—even in areas where equity is never the norm— of the programs and approaches recounted in this book. The success is primarily due to the connection of programs to the places where the schools are located and the kids live. From my perspective, the growing national and international interest in and practice of place-based education is appropriate and encouraging. This book is intended to contribute to that discussion and movement.

The associations I have formed with many rural Alabama educators, students, community members, and resource persons in this work are of great personal value. In the PACERS Small Schools Cooperative, I have especially appreciated opportunities for collaboration with committed people working beyond the call of duty and aiming to reach important and challenging goals.

I have learned from University of Alabama students engaged in and even creating programs that have benefited communities throughout the state. The students at the Wesley Foundation and those who formed the Student Coalition for Community Health (SCCH) inspired me. I am especially indebted to Dr.

Donna Jacobi Preutt, Dr. Dorothy Snoddy Murphy, and Charles "Duna" Norton. I have enjoyed my association with student mentors working out of the Program for Rural Services and Research (PRSR)—aiding schools and young people throughout rural Alabama and continuing a tradition started by the SCCH.

My colleagues at the PRSR are due much credit for the development and success of initiatives described in this book. The list is too long to include everyone, however, I especially want to acknowledge the contributions of some. Angie Wright gave good support to the SCCH and took the lead in organizing the PRSR's Community Services Project. Robin Lambert, as coordinator of the Rural Education Project, was responsible for the development and operation of the Awards Program in Writing. Without her consistent concern and initiative, the PACERS Teacher Education Program and the PACERS Cooperative would not have been created or successful. Addie Wilder and Tommie Syx made significant long-term contributions to the PACERS' Better Schools program. Andrew Goetz, Jim Wrye, Jon Chalmers, Garrett Lane, and Laura Caldwell Anderson—as students and then as PRSR staff—worked tirelessly, thoughtfully, and well to help make PACERS programs successful.

I am indebted to several persons for their help with the exemplary programs section of the book. John Harbuck and Deborah McCord, teachers responsible for successful PACERS aquaculture programs, generously took time to explain their work and its impact. In the same way Hank Fridell, Bonnie Jean Flom, and Larry Long gave me important perspectives on Elders' Wisdom and Children's Song, a process developed by Mr. Long. Jim Wrye, as coordinator of the PACERS Community Newspaper Project, shared enthusiastically his experiences in and opinions of the program. Of course, in all these projects, thanks go to the teachers who directed them, to the kids who made them work, and to the resource persons and volunteers who helped.

David Mathews's support was critical for the formation of the SCCH, and it was through his initiative that the PRSR was organized. I appreciate his interest and his insights which have helped me to understand better the implications of my work and approaches, and which continue to provide significant encouragement for the ongoing development of PACERS as an association devoted to rural schools and communities.

The generous support of the Kettering Foundation made the writing and publishing of this book possible. I am deeply grateful for that assistance. Grants from the Lyndhurst Foundation have been indispensable for programs described in this book. I am especially indebted to Jack Murrah, president of Lyndhurst, for his discernment and consistent encouragement.

Sara Day Hatton was a helpful first reader. Judy Surratt patiently made edits, corrections, and suggestions. Her advice was essential, and I am thankful for her good help. My son Rick and my wife Martha gave me time, encouragement, and needed advice. I am grateful for them and for their help.

My family connections to rural schools are strong and important. My great-grandfather was principal/teacher in small (sometimes one-room) schools, my mother was for years a rural school teacher, and my son Greg continued that tradition. These family ties have been instrumental in helping me appreciate rural schools and kids.

Jack Shelton

Westover, Alabama
March 2005

Consequential Learning

Introduction

American students are citizens of a pluralistic democratic society. They are members of specific communities that strongly inform their identity and that are essential contexts in which they learn and exercise their citizenship. They will earn their livings in a participatory economy that is increasingly information-based. Consequential Learning, the approach to school-based education advocated in this book, takes seriously all students' citizenship and their membership in communities. Accordingly, Consequential Learning aims to strengthen the capacity of schools to help students to develop these skills:

- gathering, creating, and evaluating information;
- collaborating with others to define and realize common goals;
- participating in an open economy;
- setting and realizing personal life goals; and
- exercising private and civic moral judgment.

This is a reasonable goal for public education. It encourages the development of self-aware learners. It places high value on the formation of dispositions and competencies necessary for successful individual initiative and civic action. It links learning to character formation, schools to communities, and education to a democratic way of life. Connecting public education and political governance is no easy task. In *Democratic Education,* Amy Gutmann notes that Kant identified education and government as the most difficult of human inventions.[1] Certainly, drawing them together is difficult, but attempts to promote their effective connection are essential for a democracy.

This summary is a guide for realizing the objectives of Consequential Learning elaborated throughout this book:

Consequential Learning contends that core academic and extracurricular programs of schools should routinely engage all students in the use of the concepts and tools of academic, technical, business, and artistic disciplines in order to produce beneficial public outcomes that invite direct public assessment and participation.

The goals, approaches, and programmatic formats of Consequential Learning have been developed primarily through long-term associations with students, teachers, members of rural communities, and other colleagues in the definition and implementation of programs at the University of Alabama and in rural Alabama public schools, especially those in the PACERS Cooperative.[2] Through these programs young people have demonstrated their desire and capacity to contribute to community well-being, have grown personally and academically, and have established important links to their futures. My use of the term "Consequential Learning" for the approaches presented here is not intended to suggest that other ways are without consequence. I use it because the projects from which Consequential Learning principles are derived have been praised by students, teachers, and community members for being transparently relevant to their lives and communities.

A primary purpose of this book is to help schools and

communities consider, implement, and strengthen educational approaches and programs that share the values of Consequential Learning and that improve schools and communities as well as the lives of young people. To this end I describe programs through which the approaches were developed and refined. I delineate their implications for teaching and learning. I provide guidelines and summaries of exemplary practices, and I consider related issues of educational policy and culture.

Several matters should be clarified at the outset. In criticizing educational practice and culture, I am not joining the widespread condemnation of American public schools, though I certainly do suggest that substantial reform is needed. The high dropout rate of students and the rapidly growing practice of home schooling both confirm that serious change is needed. I do not take lightly the difficulties faced by public schools, the lack of equitable support for many of them, or what they have accomplished; and I recognize that systemic reform does not come easily. In the face of existing challenges, my expectations are modest and take into consideration that a variety of changes are required if significant progress is to occur. Complex problems will not yield to single-shot methods, including standardized testing, the current prescription for healthy schools. In fact, it appears that the virtually uncontested influence of testing often makes promotion of examsmanship the only goal of schools—a limited vision of schooling at best. My argument here is not with standards or with tests, although in the current climate questioning of the absolute authority of testing is often presumed to mean indifference to standards and "accountability." To the contrary, what is generally expected of young people, including what is fostered by the most rigorous standardized testing, is far too limited to meet the needs either of students or of a democratic society.

It is too often assumed that schools are the sole agencies of instruction and that within them learning remains unconnected to the communities where their students live. However, learning takes place in more than one setting, and kids spend the great proportion of their time in non-school contexts. Their perspectives and interests are inevitably shaped by their extra-school circumstances and the places in which they live. Consequential Learning, therefore, emphasizes that communities constitute valuable instructional resources and that schools and communities must be linked to maximize student learning.

Self-determination, active learning, and entrepreneurship are central features of the educational approach recommended in this book. They suggest the high value it places on students taking initiative, becoming self-aware learners and critical thinkers capable of defining their own futures and confident that they can make a difference. They are judgments against educational practices that cultivate passivity and reminders that, as citizens and community members, students are more than receptacles for information. They warn against the potential that school has for making students academic sleep walkers, who go through the motions without understanding how school activities relate to their current or future lives. They suggest that learning is not simply the retention of information; discovering how to think and exercise critical judgment are obviously crucial. All young people in a democratic society must be expected both to become skilled at learning on their own and exercising their right to determine the accuracy and relevance of information—that is, to gain proficiencies required for informed citizenship.

Good citizenship is a matter of character and inevitably includes concern for others. Consistently in my experience, young people want to help people and to make a difference in their communities. And given the proper contexts, they work hard to do so. Kids' desire to help is an indicator of their integrity and should be fostered in schools through action. Although the impact of the ethical perspectives of elders on young people is considerable, it is important to emphasize that students have their own moral values and are ready to put them to work. Consequential Learning offers immediate opportunities for young people to contribute to the well-being of their communities, thereby, enabling them to act on and strengthen their commitments and to continue their personal and civic growth. In *Making the Grade,* Tony Wagner cites a Public Agenda survey indicating that 71 percent of all Americans believe that teaching values is more important than teaching academics.[3] In Consequential Learning the favored process for "teaching values" is akin to that used to teach driving: students learn by putting character into action.

Over time, I have arrived at three conclusions about schools which bear on this book and often surface in it directly. First, small school size is very beneficial, especially for but not limited to kids from impoverished families. My experience, as well as current research, underscores the strong positive correlations between small schools and youngsters' success.[4] By small schools I mean those with up to seventy-five students a grade, or as it was better put in a prize winning speech from a sitcom-aware fourth grader, schools that are "Cheers-size." In such schools kids are more likely to be participants than spectators, partly because small size makes the active engagement of every student essential—an important matter in effective education for a democracy where the involvement of all is to be sought. Unfortunately, driven by industrial notions and on the pretext of saving money and offering more opportunities, the size of schools has been increasing steadily.

Second, most schools are not "owned" or significantly influenced by the communities where they are located. At times it almost seems that politicians and policy makers make it their business to ensure that the public does not influence or participate in the work of schools. What appears to be asked of citizens is a willingness to pay for schools without being engaged in their operation. It is reasonable to suppose that, in the absence of significant public connections, public support will be difficult to rally even if the moment finally arrives when all students test above average.

Third, I wish Americans could routinely view the work of kids in schools. Perhaps schools should be more like my refrigerator, the true purpose of which is to display photos and artistic efforts of my grandchildren, who regularly inspect the current arrangements and comment on any changes, revealing the value they place on a public display related to their lives. It is the same for every young person. As one teacher explained in a PACERS' planning meeting, "all our kids want to shine, and we should give them the chance." PACERS projects, like those presented later as exemplary practices and like many school programs, were venues for students to produce and display handiwork significant for their communities. As could be expected: students relished the opportunities afforded by the projects; teachers gained greater local appreciation for their work; community members applauded and gave their support. Educators have always known the value of kids showing off their work. It is important for kids and public education, that they have the opportunity.

The associations and experiences on which this book is based are varied. Students involved in the projects which I helped organize and administer and on which this book is based range from affluent to very poor, and they represent a diversity of racial and ethnic groups. Their abilities, interests, and ways of knowing are equally diverse, and they have differing means of expressing their intelligence. The communities from which the students come are mainly rural, and so it's true that they share some common understanding, but nonetheless, these communities have different opportunities, resources, and histories and are as diverse as are their students. In my judgment, schools are ethically bound to honor the heterogeneity of their students. This goal does not jettison standards; it calls for teaching and learning that is community connected and for modes of instruction and evaluation that are multi-dimensional.

It is difficult for schools to tie their work to the communities where they are located given centralized governance, professionalized control, and standardized curricula and evaluation. Throughout this book, I examine the disconnect between schools and communities and between learning and place. They have negative consequences for a citizen's support and ownership of schools, for a student's motivation and learning, and for a teacher's ability to teach. The London Underground constantly warns riders to "mind the gap," that is the separation between the train and the passenger platform. Consequential Learning is mindful of the gap between schools and citizens and between the traditional goals of education and the needs of students living in a democracy with a participatory economy, and it suggests means for bridging that gap—for involving parents, community members, resource persons, businesses and agencies in the work of the school. It is possible that, wherever the gap is bridged, public schools will become sufficiently public, and, thereby, gain the civic encouragement, guidance, and support they need.

Section 1

The Inspiration for Consequential Learning

Young people are citizens and members of communities. They are capable of fulfilling responsibilities that arise from their citizenship and community membership and are prepared to do so. Given the opportunity, they will take initiative to improve the places where they live, and they will demonstrate considerably more character and grit than they are often given credit for. The principles and programs gathered under the rubric "Consequential Learning" build on young peoples' citizenship and relationships to their communities. They were imagined and refined over thirty years of work with students, work that is described and analyzed below in order to illustrate links between theory and experience and to set out guidelines and examples that will help support application of Consequential Learning principles in other situations.

The Wesley Foundation, the United Methodist Church's campus ministry at the University of Alabama, was the first setting that led me to think about the approaches in Consequential Learning. The primary constituents of the Wesley Foundation, at which I served as director, were graduate and undergraduate students, and many of them were participants in its community need programs. The second framework was the Program for Rural Services and Research (PRSR), also at the University of Alabama. The PRSR has sponsored university student projects and initiated partnerships statewide with rural schools and communities in order to engage their youngsters in ventures that enhance both learning and civic life.

As United Methodist campus minister and later as organizer and director of the PRSR, I was in a position to encourage and assist university students, to clear space for them to take initiative, and to listen to their insights and reflections. At the PRSR, the scope of my experience was extended to include many small rural public schools, where I watched kids of all ages demonstrate their interest in learning through work that connected them to their communities. My views are grounded in direct experience with students and with adults who understand young peoples' competence, commitments, and communities. The following summaries of pivotal projects are presented to document students' abilities and interests and to show how Consequential Learning was developed.

Partlow Project at the Wesley Foundation

Many of the perspectives of this book probably were set in motion by a 1968 meeting between university students and staff members at Partlow State School, Alabama's residential facility for persons then unfortunately labeled "emotionally and mentally retarded." The students were members of the Wesley Foundation attending the meeting to negotiate the terms of a service program they were keen to undertake for Partlow residents. The process had been initiated by a Partlow administrator. He was seeking to expand the opportunities available to his school's clients and asked if students at the Wesley Foundation might be interested in helping. His invitation was taken seriously and sparked a strong response—one that I have seen often when adults seek to engage young people in serious work. Students' answer to the invitation was to propose a plan that was to be reviewed at the meeting. Their proposal was imaginative, thoughtfully constructed, and placed significant responsibilities upon themselves.

The students planned a program that included events at the Wesley Foundation. Some staff members opposed the recommended program, arguing that residents did not normally leave campus, that there might be lawsuits, and that students might not be able to coordinate the effort. As other issues arose, negotiations became increasingly serious. Students held their own, pointed to potential benefits of the project, and maintained their competence to manage it. In the end, their proposal gained approval, and a groundbreaking relationship was initiated. The process was not unique. On many occasions, I have seen students make plans, establish rationales for them, and make a difference through them—a series of actions that express an intention to undertake consequential civic work that enhances communities.

For more than a decade, the program involved a large number of Partlow residents and hundreds of university students, many of whom developed individual relationships with persons from Partlow. By providing recreation, meaningful associations, and off-campus experience for residents—some of whom would eventually be placed outside the institution—the program permitted students to take on significant leadership roles. Program outcomes demonstrated benefits for all its participants—Partlow residents and students alike. However, the process of program initiation and management also began to reshape my understanding of the competencies and aspirations of young people.

The students' fundamental role in creating and advocating for the program denoted their interest in more than simply being volunteers, that is, filling existing slots. Working together, students had imagined a new plan for serving residents of Partlow and had articulated a rationale for its implementation. They made the case for a program that had systemic implications and that placed core responsibility squarely on themselves. Their planning process and negotiations with Partlow staff members were models of civic deliberation; their long-term commitment of time, money, and thought was evidence that they intended to make a difference in the community. And the program's success testified to their competence and dependability. The process defined students as citizens and community members and made clear that fulfilling the attendant responsibilities would have important consequences for their personal development and for the well-being of the place where they lived.

For more that a decade, I was privileged to help support the enterprises of University of Alabama students carried out at the Wesley Foundation. Weekly and summer-long tutorial projects, service to elders in residential facilities, tuition scholarship programs for youngsters from rural Alabama and Africa, and a big-brother volunteer initiative followed the Partlow project and reflected many of its essential features. Out of these programs, the two that most influenced my understanding of the citizenship and community membership of students were the Wesley Shelter Care Home and the Student Coalition for Community Health (SCCH).

Wesley Shelter Care Home

In the early 1970s the Juvenile Court of Tuscaloosa County requested that students at the Wesley Foundation join with it to establish and operate a residential program that would serve as an alternative to detention for adjudicated boys and girls. There were no models to follow and no operators of similar programs with whom to consult, and there were few financial resources at the court's disposal. Undaunted, Wesley Foundation students agreed to undertake the project.

Why did students attempt such a formidable task? They were not naïve about the difficulties to be faced. Their experience working with troubled youth had given them considerable insight. They knew that the situation would be volatile and unpredictable and that mistakes were inevitable. The proposed program would demand much of their time and would place them in situations requiring constant attention and accountability. Students often explained that they accepted the challenge primarily because they were asked to do so. The request, actually a challenge, honored their ability and concern; it counted upon them to continue to make a difference in the life of the community. The stereotypes of university students were not applied to the Wesley group. The offer of partnership denoted respect that was compelling.

Another reason that students accepted the challenge was that, as big brothers and sisters, they already knew and were concerned about boys and girls under court jurisdiction. Social problems and the persons debilitated by them were not abstractions for these young people; they had seen them and had come to believe that they could help. The students had already worked with officers of the court and had collaborated with their peers to address community needs. They not only had served as volunteers, they had created a program through which others could help kids who needed a big brother or sister. Their history of effective public work also gave them confidence needed to make a positive response to the court's request.

Finally, students agreed to see the project through because they are persons of character, whose belief systems and civic understandings engendered commitment and determination. There are two primary emphases in Consequential Learning that are rooted in this final explanation of why students would agree to assume such responsibilities. First, Consequential Learning affirms that kids have character, that they are capable of making informed commitments, and they should be called upon to do so. Rather than being blank tablets waiting to have virtues inscribed on them, they are individuals ready to be tested and to demonstrate their convictions. There is no suggestion here that character development ever ceases or that any person, young or old, ever has it all figured out. The point is to realize that young people are neither moral voids nor moral deficits and that their characters are strengthened by action. Second, in the Shelter Care work, their commitments, and the actions emanating from them, were strengthened through association with adults involved in the project as professionals or as volunteers. It was highly beneficial for students to know and be known by adults and to receive their affirmation and guidance. The approaches and projects of Consequential Learning value the creation of meaningful settings through which young people and adults can learn from and about each other.

Working with representatives of the court, especially its chief officer, John Upchurch, students energetically began the process of acquiring and renovating physical facilities; working out the logistics of supervision, feeding, and transportation; meeting the codes of various governmental agencies; and fashioning an operational program. Because the Shelter Care work offered valuable career-related experience, Wesley students were soon joined by their peers in social work, psychology, and other fields related to the program. As with the Partlow project and the efforts described below, students demonstrated their capacity to identify and to create contexts of consequence for their learning.

Churches, civic organizations, and individuals in the community contributed time, expertise, money, furnishings, and building materials needed to implement the Shelter Care project. Local people offered a great deal of assistance when they saw the students' commitment and public work. It became clear that adults are ready to help and encourage young people when the settings for action are available. I came to believe, as a correlative, that support for public schools declines when citizens cannot see what is going on or understand how they can be of benefit to the institutions and to the kids.

Younger students in the community contributed as well—on their own, junior high school kids held fund-raisers for the homes. Their gifts of money and affirmation were significant motivators for the Shelter Care organizers and were indicators of the community interest of young people whose work presaged similar contributions made by rural youngsters through the programs of the PACERS Cooperative and other school-based ventures described below.

It never occurred to me that the students would fail to fulfill the responsibilities of their partnership with the court. They had been asked to undertake the project because of their track record in working with adjudicated youth and in creating and sustaining other community projects. Students were instrumental in purchasing and remodeling facilities and in preparing an operation manual, as well as staffing and running the program. They did all this in close association with officers of the court and a full-time supervisor. Serving hundreds of adjudicated youth who would otherwise have been held in detention, the program operated for four years; because it proved its value as an alternative to detention, it was subsequently adopted and operated by local government. The students had met the expectations of the juvenile court and their work had demonstrated their civic ability and their community membership.

Student Coalition for Community Health

Experience with the Shelter Care program and other initiatives gave Wesley students the skills and confidence necessary to organize in the mid-1970s the Student Coalition for Community Health (SCCH), an organization that for twenty-five years formed effective partnerships with rural Alabamians to improve community and individual health and to enhance educational and personal growth. The experiences and reflections of SCCH participants expanded my understanding of students' citizenship and community membership and have been especially important in the development of Consequential Learning approaches.

Modeled on the Student Health Coalition operating out of the Center for Health Services at Vanderbilt University, the SCCH was built upon the hopes, the competence, and the persistence of Wesley Foundation members joined by other University of Alabama students, especially from the New College, an innovative academic unit that permitted students to take a great deal of initiative in their own education. In addition, students from universities and medical schools around the country were employed on health fair staffs. Young people signed up with the SCCH primarily to make a difference in the well-being of rural Alabama communities. Those whose only objective was resumé building were not well received—more was expected than getting the jump on peers in the quest for scarce slots in medical schools. In preparation SCCH students observed and worked as staff members in Vanderbilt's health fairs, which they were seeking to adapt to Alabama. Through these fairs, graduate and undergraduate students, living with community members and receiving support from Vanderbilt faculty and other professionals, conducted comprehensive screening clinics in inner-city Nashville as well as in rural communities in the mountains of east Tennessee and in the western, cotton-growing area of the state. The health fairs were appealing to Alabama students, who grasped their potential to provide medical services while promoting community organization essential for long-term improvements. With crucial assistance from Bill Dow and others at Vanderbilt, students began the hard work of organizing, recruiting, fund-raising, and proposal writing; forming partnerships with communities; and making essential connections with individuals and agencies needed to provide guidance and support.

The road was not easy. Tasks were complex and costly in terms of students' time, energy, and even their personal cash flow. Not being taken seriously, however, especially by some medical professionals and agency administrators, was the most difficult problem for students. It sapped their energy even though it was counterbalanced by remarkable support from many professionals, especially William Willard and John Packard of the College of Community Health Sciences at the University of Alabama.

Once I accompanied an SCCH member meeting with a health agency director for the purpose of interpreting the initial health fair programs and requesting support. Before the student could complete her brief presentation, the director pronounced the program a waste of time and suggested that she volunteer to file articles, reports, and journals in the agency office. It was a revealing response, clearly stating that the director felt there was no reason even to find out anything about the student, a recent honors graduate of the University of Alabama on her way to Vanderbilt's school of medicine with considerable scholarship support. Her well thought-out career aspirations were service-based and in line with the agency's mandates, but the director was unwilling to engage her or to listen to her presentation of a program to which she was obviously committed. Unfortunately this was not the only occasion on which I saw young persons and their aspirations dismissed without a hearing.

In forming the SCCH and preparing for its first health fair project, students faced a variety of crises mainly centered on the establishment of partnerships with communities, agencies, professionals, and funders. The project had no track record, and it was being promoted by college students who were asking a lot. Inevitably there were ups and downs that required students to be persistent and smart. The most critical of the problems was a last-minute change in requirements by the Robert Wood Johnson Foundation (RWJ), the major initial source of financial support. The foundation determined that funds would have to be routed through the University of Alabama and not the Wesley Foundation as originally specified. The change placed students in a difficult situation. The Wesley Foundation Board of Directors had assured students that, within normal organizational rules, they would be the decision-makers regarding the expenditure of grant funds. The turn of events left them without that assurance. After hours of difficult deliberation in a meeting to decide their course of action, SCCH student members decided overwhelmingly to reject the grant and cancel their plans. In order to insure the integrity of their organization, they were willing to turn down indispensable financial resources, face up to their failure with community members and other supporters, and lose summer jobs in which they had invested a great deal—including a substantial amount of hope. They understood that their decision put the SCCH in serious jeopardy; but they had taken responsibility for the project, and it would succeed or fail under their leadership. Whether the decision was right or wrong, it demonstrated character and a willingness to sacrifice for principle.

The decision and the process whereby it was made shaped the organization. Students had tested their commitment and had demonstrated their belief in their own competence. Ultimately, through the intervention of David Mathews, president of the University of Alabama, and Neal Berte, dean of its New College, arrangements were made that allowed students to take the responsibilities they sought, accept the RWJ funding, and proceed with their work. Both Mathews and Berte were committed to having students take initiative and assume civic responsibility. The university provided administrative support requisite for SCCH success, facilitated student decision making, and matched the existing commitments of the Wesley Foundation. The efforts of the SCCH made a significant difference to students and to many people and communities in the state, thereby furthering the goals of the supporting institutions that maintained their own organizational integrity while fostering the creation of new contexts where young people could grow in character, prepare for their futures, and understand more clearly the relevance of their education.

With funding from the Robert Wood Johnson Foundation and the United Methodist Church and with support from the University of Alabama and the Wesley Foundation, SCCH students set about implementing their first health fairs in three rural Alabama communities. Living with community members who provided room and board, students offered free comprehensive health assessments; they were assisted by physicians, nurses and nurse practitioners, hospitals and health agencies, medical, nursing, and optometry schools, local health departments, and several university departments. Screening clinics were usually set up in schools and were operated at times that were accessible even to persons working night shifts. The hours were long and the work difficult, but growing awareness of the seriousness of local health problems confirmed they were doing the right thing.

Students also valued the health fairs for the personal development opportunities they offered, and this reinforced their commitment to the SCCH. The preparation done by its founding students was insightful and thorough and laid the groundwork for future accomplishments. Over time SCCH effectiveness correlated with student leadership, funding levels, community response, and the support of agencies and individuals. In the judgment of external evaluators, community members and the students themselves, the SCCH was highly successful and provided a history that warrants reflection.

There are two questions about the SCCH that are especially relevant for understanding Consequential Learning: What happened as a result of students' efforts? What values and interests did these efforts reveal? The first question focuses on the organization and its activities as a context for student learning, personal development, and effective civic action. The second examines motivations and aspirations.

What did the health fairs and the SCCH achieve? In the first place, students learned a lot. They developed and applied a variety of skills, many of which related to their college majors and their potential careers. Medical students learned how to take patient histories, give screening exams, and begin to trust their own judgment; social work students gained knowledge about the functioning of communities and the operation of government agencies; and history students occasionally chronicled local life. Participants also developed civic capacities: SCCH student coordinators became skilled at organizing; public speaking and interpretation built the confidence of most members; collaborative decision making, problem solving, and action were routine; and students learned how to take stock of their efforts in demanding and complex circumstances.

Students sought and gained considerable first-hand perspective on health systems and on individual health. They became conversant with the sources of many of the state's health problems. Some learned why they were interested in being medical professionals and others that they wanted no part of medicine. SCCH work gave participants a chance to study their state and to appreciate the value of the knowledge of place. They made friends, often across racial and cultural lines, and they had fun doing so. Their self-esteem was bolstered by the gratitude and affirmation they received from community members. Students were pleased that they had tested their values and resolve and had proved their capacity to make a difference.

Many members considered their SCCH experience to be the most important in their education and in their personal growth. I regard that assessment as particularly significant, since students in the formative years of the SCCH were not afraid to pass negative judgments on their own efforts or those of their peers. Consequential Learning's emphasis on young peoples' attention to self-evaluation is grounded in its benefits for SCCH students who made the case that they were entitled to judge their lives for themselves. Students—who are citizens—are not often encouraged to carry out their responsibility to assess the contexts and content of their education. As a result, it often seems that they are conditioned to focus primarily on what they must do to obtain the grades they want.

The health fairs also produced benefits for community

members—many of which they would not otherwise have enjoyed. Thousands of people were screened and tested, and previously undiscovered pathologies were revealed. A number of them were life-threatening and were treated by physicians and hospitals that had agreed to receive health-fair referrals. Communities remembered the life-altering and life-saving cases. They influenced peoples' attitudes toward their own health care and engendered an appreciation for the SCCH; and they were the foundation for partnerships later created between the University of Alabama and rural communities in the state.

I was routinely told by community participants in the health fairs that their physical exams were the best they had ever had. Although supervising physicians frequently questioned such valuations, it was agreed that people were responding positively to the thoroughness with which medical and nursing students explained the examination process. They also provided useful information on healthy living and on how to make connections with local or regional health agencies. Through the administration of medical histories and SCCH-designed community health surveys, and through physical examinations, water testing, and demographic studies, SCCH members collected significant local information as well and used the results to foster local improvement.

With energy and insight, SCCH members gathered, analyzed, interpreted, and acted on information. As a result of that practice, the SCCH provided community members good information for community health planning and projects. Most important for Consequential Learning was the confirmation of the eagerness and capacity of young people to gather and apply relevant information.

Young community members assisted in the health fairs and, thereby, established important connections with university students. In a joking but revealing assessment, they noted that if the health fair staff members could succeed in college and in professional careers, so could they. For many rural youngsters these kinds of connections were unique and valuable. In the process it was made clear to me that young people in school, especially kids with limited connections and options, would find association with undergraduate and graduate students very profitable. In the projects described below, this notion was continually reaffirmed, both by university students returning to their schools as mentors and through the participation of adult resource persons.

Positive outcomes for individual students and community members were important objectives for the health fairs. More often than not, however, project success was measured by systemic changes. Students worked hard to insure that the results of the fairs included permanent local improvements, and SCCH activities were, in fact, pivotal to the creation of numerous primary health care clinics and other additions to community infrastructure, such as libraries, playgrounds, parks, and water systems.

The SCCH is a success story with respect to community institutional change, but its experience is also a reminder that, whether in a major university or in a rural school, reform occurs infrequently and seems extremely difficult to sustain. The SCCH's twenty-five year run was certainly unanticipated, and its accomplishments—including systemic changes—also exceeded expectation. Yet, despite its success, the organization could never garner the institutional respect and support it needed to fulfill its potential or to become a permanent entity. When external private funding had been exhausted, university commitments to match the unfailing contributions of rural communities were not forthcoming. Although that may simply have been result of insufficient institutional revenue, it remains a reminder that educational reform is a complex long-term undertaking for which the "funding plumbing" has usually not been laid.

It is important to emphasize again that the efforts of SCCH students brought about lasting systemic changes. In addition to the establishment of local clinics and other infrastructure additions, the University of Alabama, based on the SCCH, created a program to connect the institution to rural communities. The achievements of the SCCH testify to the capacity of young people, when appropriately challenged and supported, to recognize and address even deep-seated systemic problems. But, the ability to effect change is not peculiar to university students. Reference will be made later to the work of rural public school students who significantly contributed to improving the infrastructure of their communities and counties.

What motivated SCCH students? With several exceptions, students in the SCCH were diligent and thoughtful in the planning and implementation of demanding projects in which a great deal was at stake and whose outcomes were very public. During the period of the first health fairs, students spent considerable time assessing the quality of their efforts, the impact of their work on communities, and their own personal development. Observing their work, listening to their group discussions, and interviewing students individually permitted me to gain perspective on what mattered most to them and what motivated them to undertake and complete difficult tasks.

The young people who established the SCCH placed the highest priority on making a difference in the lives of communities. Although "making a difference" is perhaps a cliché, it does summarize what drove students more than anything else. For some, it suggested traditional community service, but for others it meant improving the prospects of rural communities and even improving health-care policies and the university itself.

The SCCH was a student-created venue in which young people could make critical decisions, take responsibility, and actualize their commitment to self-determination. It was important to students that outcomes be, to a great degree, in their hands—from that priority much of the energy and success of the SCCH was derived. An interesting by-product of the new leadership opportunities offered by the SCCH was the extensive participation of women, who in disproportionate numbers assumed the crucial role of project coordinator and made up a majority of the staff membership. Female students have also participated in significant numbers and taken leadership roles in other programs described in this book, suggesting that programs linked to community improvement can create opportunities that are especially equitable and inclusive.

SCCH members' interest in taking responsibility was balanced by their commitment to forming partnerships. Collaboration was seen as an essential component of success, and it was understood that compromise would occasionally be required. Students sought to become partners with professionals, agencies, and communities, but they wanted to be viewed as responsible agents in the health fair projects. At times. professionals associated with the SCCH mistook their insistence on assuming responsibility and making decisions for arrogance when it was, in fact, prerequisite to the formation of equal partnerships. From the outset, SCCH students refused to look upon the health fairs as their sole possession. They were undertaken and carried out in partnership with communities and were regarded as mutually beneficial.

Because of their potential for enhancing community life, students sometimes measured the outcomes of health fairs by the formation of new associations within communities and between communities and individuals and organizations. The word "coalition" in the organization's title was early evidence of students' interest in partnerships and their recognition of the value of cooperation with communities and with the persons and agencies committed to them. The use of partnerships to effect public improvements is a persistent theme in Consequential Learning because they are fundamental to civic life and to successful community action. In the same way because of their ability to extend institutional resources and capacities, it is also apparent that the effective education of young people requires the collaboration of individuals and organizations outside the schools. The SCCH proclivity for establishing collaborative relationships was an important backdrop to the formation of the PACERS Cooperative and other rural partnerships needed to support change agendas.

Students were looking for real world experience, and they found it. They were sure they needed more than a classroom education and were eager to learn from people whose experiences differed from their own and those of their teachers. During the summer-long health fairs, students often lived and worked in circumstances wrought by desperate poverty. For most of them the experience of pervasive need was unknown; for some it was going home. In either case they brought a self-imposed mandate to partner with people and communities in need to improve the welfare of both. Students often had to deal with the effects of racism and depressed rural economies, circumstances that tested their resolve. On the other hand, they found some communities that were on the rise, ready to take important steps and looking for the kind of boost the SCCH could provide.

Members of the SCCH were welcomed into local homes,

where they were treated as family, regarded as persons with skills, and accepted as friends across racial, cultural, and economic lines. Students had sought such experiences and thrived on the opportunities they afforded—opportunities that they created for themselves but that were enriched by the way rural Alabama communities welcomed them, worked with them, and taught them. The acceptance of students by communities exemplifies the willingness of adults to support young people and to enhance their education and personal experience, provided they have a context for doing so.

SCCH students sought real world experience in part to facilitate career preparation. Nursing, medical, law, and optometry students were looking for hands on experience, and undergraduate students were trying out their interests. The health fairs and projects derived from them were not, however, exclusively medical; they called for persons with skills in community organizing, social work, education, and the arts. The fairs were interdisciplinary and allowed students to share interests in ways not usually provided by standard academic fare. They were quick to cross disciplinary lines or the boundaries separating the various medical specialties. Sharing the goal of making a difference, students learned from and supported each other as they explored their future prospects.

Students were interested in learning about rural Alabama, and they understood that without knowledge of the communities where they would be working, they would not be working very well. So they placed matters of demography, geography, politics, and economics on the agenda for health fair staff orientation sessions. Residents were asked for information and for stories that would shed light on their communities. Understanding that local knowledge was crucial for organizing the fairs effectively; students were well aware of the power of place.

The SCCH demonstrated students' desire and capacity to take responsibility for making a difference and for creating means to enhance their education, to prepare for their future, and to learn about the world and their place within it. They manifested the will to form partnerships, to work hard and to work together, to be serious and to have fun, and to learn from professionals who supported their efforts and from community members who sometimes became their friends. Students set high goals and held themselves to high standards. The SCCH was an exercise in citizenship, and it helped young people fulfill important aspirations: to learn about themselves and their state, to begin to master the practices by which they would earn their livings, to know and work with adults in collegial relationships, and to make a significant difference. These aspirations have been embodied in the work of the Program for Rural Services and Research and in the approaches I have labeled "Consequential Learning."

Program for Rural Services and Research

A model of productive university and rural community collaboration, the SCCH engendered the creation of the Program for Rural Services and Research at the University of Alabama, which was designed to make the resources and capacities of the institution accessible to communities through mutually beneficial partnerships aimed at enhancing rural well-being. From the outset, it has been obvious that schools are crucial to rural community development and that they have to be partners of the PRSR if its mandate is to be fulfilled. Within its overall program, the PRSR has established a rural education focus that resulted in the Awards Program in Writing (APW), the PACERS Cooperative, and other school initiatives that are primary subjects of this book.

The work of the SCCH was indispensable to the PRSR's success: relationships the organization had created with rural communities and schools enabled the PRSR to begin to form effective partnerships throughout rural Alabama; in addition, the SCCH had garnered the long-term support of the Lyndhurst Foundation, without which the program could not have undertaken its rural education initiatives.

The PRSR began, then, with approaches, partnerships, and backing derived from the efforts of students and their supporters. Processes developed by the SCCH have been replicated in PRSR initiatives, some of which are described below.

Awards Program in Writing

The APW, a multiyear PRSR project undertaken annually during the 1980s in several small but diverse rural public schools, provided opportunities for students to publish writings about their lives and their communities. Guidelines required that all members of participating classes prepare an essay, a poem, and a brief piece of fiction and that at least one selection from each student had to be included in the published collection. PRSR staff and University of Alabama MFA students served as "first audiences" and provided technical help for the young writers and were resource persons for teachers. Participants included classes of students (primarily tenth graders) in schools representing a broad ethnic and economic spectrum of rural Alabama.

APW processes and outcomes embodied perspectives that underpin Consequential Learning and helped inform later PRSR school-related initiatives. Every student in every participating class—except a few youngsters with learning disabilities—met the writing requirements. To be sure, the quality of writing varied, but all students demonstrated an ability to select and use words expressively. Their work very often exceeded teacher expectations. The APW proved to be a context in which those who were often expected to struggle did very well. In short, both the likely and unlikely were writers. This outcome runs counter to the prevailing view of post-secondary instructors and employers, that young people cannot write and read.

What occurred? First, young people were asked to write about themselves, their families, and their communities. The process was completely grounded in students' lives and called upon them to describe what they knew well and cared about most. Using language to explore and communicate perspectives on their own experience was motivating and helped students to write. Mentors and PRSR staff members assisted those who were stymied by asking them to talk about grandparents, family reunions, fishing and hunting or their responsibilities at home, and other matters of likely interest. Students usually responded with interesting details and insights that they subsequently transferred to paper, as they came to realize that their lives and thoughts were of interest to others.

Second, students were writing for an audience beyond their teachers and even beyond their schools. Hundreds of copies of the anthologies were printed, distributed, and added to school libraries, including their own; and their written work was unveiled in well-attended local ceremonies. Students were highly motivated by the prospect of having a public audience, one that would see their names in print and that would have a stake in their work. Their communities would be engaged with what they wrote: in effect, their membership in those communities became a factor in their learning.

Third, students, teachers, and "outsiders" with technical capacity worked together to produce a consequential public outcome. Because all three "parties" had a stake in the process and all would be measured by its results, collaboration and trust were built. The triad of students, teachers, and outsiders proved to be effective over time and became a central element of Consequential Learning.

Fourth, the PRSR created space and an opportunity for schools and teachers to undertake projects that would not otherwise have been possible. PRSR funding assistance, expertise, and validation proved essential to attracting and holding the schools' interest in the project, again underscoring the need for external involvement of resource agencies as well as communities in efforts to improve education.

The APW made it necessary for students to work together in a process that required both critical judgment and compromise. Students were fully engaged in the selection of writings to be included in the collections. There was give-and-take over what would be published and how the publications would be organized and designed. On a few occasions, the responsibility for editing and arranging the text was entirely in the hands of students owing primarily to changes in teacher assignments. As with the PACERS Community Newspaper Project described below, students' placed high value upon design as well as content in order to insure that their work was presented in an attractive and representative format.

The APW was crucial in helping to define approaches followed in Consequential Learning. It demonstrated the potential of external individuals and agencies for augmenting the learning opportunities provided by schools. Its success proved that work linked to a public beyond the school has immense instructional and motivational value and should be included in students' experience. The APW strengthened existing relationships between the PRSR and rural Alabama schools and communities or created new ones, and it helped pave the way for the

PACERS Cooperative and Better Schools Building Better Communities, its program of school and community enhancement.

PACERS Small Schools Cooperative

The PACERS Cooperative was organized as an association of about thirty small public schools representing the economic, ethnic, and geographical diversity of rural Alabama. Under the pressure of a relentless state-led education policy and practice resulting in school closures, the cooperative was formed to keep schools open by demonstrating their viability and to build on their strengths in order to improve their students' prospects. It seeks to fulfill its goal of "keeping alive and getting better" through several means, among them, using appropriate digital technology for instruction, communication, and information access; offering new and relevant curricular and extracurricular opportunities; and developing entrepreneurial skills and dispositions. With the support of private foundations and governmental agencies, the association has implemented a comprehensive program of educational and community improvement. It has made the case for small schools in an effort both to persuade policy makers of their value and to stem the tide of closures.

The PRSR was instrumental in forming the PACERS Cooperative for reasons similar to the goals of Consequential Learning. In the first instance, the PRSR mandate to assist in the development of rural communities meant that support of schools had to be central. Rural schools and rural communities are symbiotic, and their mutual interdependence calls for their mutual support. It is generally acknowledged that rural schools are the heart of their communities and that the demise of these schools often presages the demise of the communities they serve. After all, schools are often a community's largest employer, bringing professional expertise and providing important local identity. But the dependence of schools on communities has not been very well understood, with the result that an unfortunate disconnect often develops between the two—weakening both. In any case, the PRSR mandate has made helping schools and linking them more closely to their communities central elements of its agenda.

PRSR staff were also committed to the formation of a statewide association of small rural schools because collaboration promised more external support and programmatic success than individual single-shot efforts. The pragmatic commitment to partnership is an essential element of Consequential Learning given that systemic change is more likely to be influenced by strong networks and by the evidence derived from similar work carried out in diverse settings. The disjunction between schools and communities may not have been an intended outcome of educational policy, however, it is deep-seated reality. I do not believe that it can be reversed only by discrete local efforts that may accelerate existing competition among schools that may have been exacerbated by pervasive standardized testing.

The chief PACERS program is Better Schools Building Better Communities, whose development has been significant in defining the approaches and formats of Consequential Learning. Initially, PRSR staff and representatives from each participating school got together for planning sessions, which called upon teachers, administrators, and in some cases local residents to consider the strengths of their schools and communities and to imagine ways to link them through curricular and extracurricular programs. The aspirations of teachers were emphasized, creating difficulties for some experienced teachers who felt their best efforts had been consistently thwarted and who were, therefore, reluctant to put forward their hopes. Nonetheless, the meetings proved to be energizing—focusing deliberately on strengths and visions, they gave little attention to educational pathologies and fix-it strategies. They elicited the contributions of teachers as competent creative professionals and asked them to act on their own understanding of students, teaching, and local communities. The meetings also opened up discussions of individual school histories. Short on nostalgia, reflections about the past recalled meaningful contributions of schools to local life—plays, musical evenings, strong home economics and agriculture programs, and service initiatives through which students provided assistance to community members.

Following the initial planning meetings at each site, interested teachers were asked to propose projects that would build upon local capacities, link learning to place, and add to students' curricular and extracurricular opportunities. Teachers presented their proposals at "cluster" meetings of representatives from four or five schools. These were often rewritten in light of responses received and/or presentations made by other schools. This interschool professional collaboration was a dominant aspect of the planning process. The well-articulated aspirations of their peers motivated teachers to improve their proposals and to believe that they could be implemented. Good ideas moved quickly through the PACERS network, and teachers began to feel that an excellent form of professional development was providing themselves opportunities to work together to find new ways of improving their practice and serving their students and schools.

The revised proposals of all the schools were literally placed on the table at a PACERS planning conference. Teachers, administrators, and PRSR staff and consultants melded them into a program format called Better Schools Building Better Communities, made up of three components: Genius of Place, Sustaining Communities, and Joy. The program encompasses a variety of projects carried out at multiple sites. Oral history, photography, and community newspaper ventures are among those developed in the Genius of Place category. Through projects initiated under the Sustaining Communities rubric, students in PACERS schools have helped prepare, administer, and evaluate health inventories and economic surveys; they were instrumental in establishing a variety of school-based enterprises and operated "living labs" (e.g. aquaculture units) and print shops; and they built solar houses and greenhouses as well as computers and computer networks. Sustaining Communities projects called for development of the means to teach entrepreneurship and support the establishment of student-run businesses. Inclusion of the Joy component constituted an important statement that schools that have a lot to celebrate, and celebration characterizes much of Better Schools Building Better Communities. Students in almost all PACERS elementary schools have participated in Elder's Wisdom and Children's Song (an exemplary practice described below) and others in plays about local subjects. An emphasis on good literature and the joy of reading led to the widespread implementation of the Book Shows project, an initiative that had been piloted by the PRSR in several schools. This project has been a means for elementary teachers to acquire excellent books for their classes both to read and to use as models for their own creative activities. The volumes have proved especially valuable to teachers helping students write their own books, produce their own illustrations, and prepare plays and skits.

Better Schools Building Better Communities projects have stretched the capacities of schools and teachers. They require outside resource persons; they have introduced new technologies as means to address real needs, and made it necessary for students and teachers to participate in intensive training workshops. Nature trails, greenhouses, aquaculture units and fish ponds, photography labs, and buildings to house new projects have been constructed. Existing spaces have been modified to accommodate newspaper publishing and other new student-run school-based enterprises. Opportunities for computer-based instruction and resource sharing have been created, and these add significantly to students' options. The public and beneficial outcomes of the program engage communities and other support constituencies in the life of schools. Students pursued new career opportunities through projects that connected them to professionals and allowed them to begin practicing the rudiments of work in such areas as publishing, construction, and aquaculture.

The PACERS Cooperative is the result of entrepreneurship: persons and institutions seeking to improve rural schools and communities joined together to form an association through which they could act in creative ways. It is important to stress that PACERS was not organized simply to ensure that rural schools get their fair share of educational resources. From the outset, its members and supporters have been determined to create new approaches and learning opportunities. To be sure, they are aware that small rural schools lacked resources that are readily available in more affluent settings, but they are even more aware of the need to use their own resources and knowledge to make their kids' education more effective and relevant. Entrepreneurial notions were operative in the formation of PACERS; and not surprisingly, they still hold a central place in the cooperative's objectives and programs.

The creation of school-based enterprises was on the minds of teachers, administrators, and students during the initial planning of PACERS, with two principal results. More than forty such ventures were initiated across the state, and support for the development of entrepreneurial skills and dispositions was formalized through AlabamaREAL—a PRSR program that offers teachers entrepreneurial training, helps schools initiate and operate student businesses, and links teachers and students involved in entrepreneurial activities.

The widespread interest in entrepreneurial initiatives throughout PACERS has demonstrated that, when given the opportunity, many educators want to teach in ways that are entrepreneurial and that promote students' capacity to take initiative for their futures. Likewise, when young people have a chance to assume the kinds of responsibilities required in entrepreneurial programs, they will do so. And there are public and private organizations as well as professionals and community members ready to help when schools seek to implement entrepreneurial education and opportunities. Several PACERS entrepreneurial ventures focusing on computer technology are illustrative.

During the planning of Better Schools, Rick Clifton, a teacher at Cedar Bluff High School in Cherokee County, wanted computers for his students. Recognizing that the private supporters of PACERS were not in the business of giving away computers, he realized that what he needed was the resources that would enable kids to build their own. And so, Tiger Computers was born; and, through this venture, students began assembling and repairing computers and running a business that grossed hundreds of thousands of dollars during some years of its operation. With Clifton's assistance, they laid the groundwork for an association with TDS, a major national communications company, that resulted in the installation of the first Internet server in Cherokee County—probably the first anywhere in rural Alabama. Access to Internet technology improved the county's prospect of attracting new industry and increased the ability of local entrepreneurs to operate in the emerging information economy.

Tiger Computers did not survive, but it left an important legacy that reflects basic Consequential Learning principles. Its story, well-documented by the media, confirmed the power of young people, teachers, and schools to initiate enterprises that strongly benefit local communities. The career-related choices of many of the students involved in Tiger Computers showed how such enterprises can link young people to their futures. The company's ability to design and operate a cost-effective network that enabled school and public libraries to share information resources was a precursor to later on-line resources developed by the PRSR and the state. Tiger fostered a disposition to build and create, which is indispensable for citizens intent on taking initiative, and even risk, to make their own way or to make their communities better places. That disposition basic to Tiger was transferred by a Tiger alum and PRSR staff member who helped students in Hale County, Alabama, establish NuGeneration Technologies.

NuGenerations, a project of the Hale County school system and AlabamaREAL, received strong start-up support from the Appalachian Regional Commission's Entrepreneurship Initiative. Like Tiger Computers and many other PACERS enterprises, NuGenerations has taken on tough and consequential assignments. One of them was to wire the hundred-year-old county courthouse to provide connectivity within the building as well as Internet access. It might be said that the students of NuGenerations, armed with skills, determination, and professional mentors brought their county into the information age.

Like the students with whom I worked in the 1970s, those who run NuGenerations and those participating in many other

PACERS projects have demonstrated the motivation and capacity of young people to make a significant difference in their communities and to learn and grow in challenging contexts related to the places where they live. The projects also reveal the power of local teachers, administrators, resource persons, and community members to imagine better ways to educate their kids. The remainder of this book is intended to help those persons and agencies who wish to challenge young people by offering them new and effective ways to strengthen their citizenship, to express their membership in communities, and to become better equipped to live their lives.

Section 2

CONSEQUENTIAL LEARNING PRINCIPLES

The principles of Consequential Learning have been derived from successful long-term programs in rural Alabama, including those of the Student Coalition for Community Health, the Community Services Project, the Awards Program in Writing,[1] and especially the PACERS Better Schools Building Better Communities program-. These initiatives have prompted some fundamental changes at state and local levels in education and community development practices. And the insightful reflections of participants on their work have been instrumental in helping me to define Consequential Learning's standards and strategies. I have also learned from the efforts of rural education organizations, researchers, and practitioners elsewhere in the United States and in Australia, Norway, and Canada.

Consequential Learning principles are interrelated and overlapping. They are strongly influenced by what I have identified as the appropriate goal of education for democratic citizenship—developing students' ability to access and evaluate information, to collaborate with others, to participate in the economy, and to exercise moral judgment. Consequential Learning promotes the notion that young people strengthen their citizenship by putting it into action. It offers teachers and schools alternatives to prevailing practice, alternatives that create connections with local constituencies normally excluded from governance and that present public evidence of institutional competence and goals. These inevitably imply particular means for improving schools and reforming educational practice.

Comprehensive Student Responsibilities

Consequential Learning assigns students complex responsibilities, and the success of the projects requires that they deliver. My confidence in young people is derived from observing them, implementing programs with them, and evaluating the results of their efforts. I have also been convinced by teachers, community members, and resource persons who have trusted that students would respond to difficult challenges and whose confidence has been confirmed by the outcomes of Consequential Learning projects. Many educators fully expect that their students' will carry out serious public work; for others, the projects often provide a new and fuller perspective on the ability and inclination of young people to assume responsibility.

Because Consequential Learning projects do not conform to the classroom mold, educators sometimes assume that they are inappropriate contexts for learning. As the descriptions of exemplary practices make clear, youngsters are challenged to acquire and apply information that frequently goes beyond what is transmitted in traditional school programs. All students are expected to be active learners, to grasp important concepts, and to demonstrate their understanding of them.

Decision Making. Decision making is among the central responsibilities of students, and they are expected to be participants in the planning, implementation, assessment, and interpretation of projects. As decision makers, they are called upon to use their intelligence and to express their own judgments. The juxtaposition of acumen and free will, sometimes traced to Plato, is essential in a participatory democracy. Taking instructions and following them are primary elements of conventional education; making decisions and setting standards are not. The former are essentially passive while the latter are active expressions of independent thought. Students are encouraged to see themselves as decision makers and are given opportunities to reflect on the consequences of their deliberation. Consequential Learning strategies call for students, teachers, and schools to take initiative, to be entrepreneurial, and to change the education culture from passive to active. Decision making involves both active learning and critical thinking; it is an important means by which students manifest agency and take initiative.

Using Tools and Concepts. Students are expected to master disciplinary tools and concepts and to use them to produce outcomes that have public consequences for themselves and their communities. Tools may be physical, such as graphic design software, or conceptual, such as protocols for oral history interviews.

There are good reasons to position students to use such tools. Tools are essential to producers. Hearing that Home Economics is now called Consumer Science, I was reminded that students are generally expected to be consumers more than producers or creators, and they are tested primarily on their consumptive rather than their productive capacities. Random-access memory counts for a lot in an education culture whose highest priority is learning discrete, subject-based facts generated by the various disciplines and generally transmitted by textbooks and lectures. It is a relatively passive process that emphasizes recalling a particular date, for example, but places little value on understanding the conceptual tools by which it is identified and given significance.

In Consequential Learning projects, students have the opportunity to move from being recipients of information (often unconnected to their lives and interests) to being its creators. By filling the role of scientist or historian and by using the tools and techniques of the trade, they can become better learners. There is a vast difference between training for the recall of assorted facts on a test and development of intellectual frameworks for the creation and analysis of information. Learning to use concepts and tools gives students priceless skills, and enhances their ability to think critically and solve problems, which is essential to democratic citizenship in an information-based society.

Helping students use professional, industrial, and disciplinary tools and concepts often requires that schools seek the assistance of persons with skills and experience not found among their faculty members. The capacity of schools is thereby enlarged, and students gain valuable opportunities to learn from and work with adults who make their livings using those tools and concepts. The result is collaboration across generational lines in order to achieve common and consequential goals. This collaboration helps bridge the gap between young people and adults doing "adult work," which Deborah Meier sees as the "central educational dilemma of our times."[2]

Schools do not usually expect students to use disciplinary instruments and principles and some educators may find the idea problematical. The PACERS Community Newspaper Project (PCNP) has experienced a few difficulties related to student use of tools and concepts. Through the PCNP, youngsters produce newspapers for communities that have no local media. To do so, they must become journalists and publishers and use computers and a range of industry level software. These costly tools are not standard fare in schools with limited resources and most principals and teachers relish the opportunities that such equipment creates for their students. On the other hand, some project directors have restricted its use to themselves or one or two kids. They have been concerned that the equipment might be damaged or that students might not use it properly; the expensive hardware and software belong to an unfamiliar digital world. I appreciate that *new* and *expensive* are not to be taken lightly in under-funded schools; students, however, have proved to be competent, quick to learn, and aware of the need to care for the equipment when they have a clear and relevant task to complete through its use.

Another concern involves the new status of students. In a project as demanding as the PCNP, it is almost inevitable that they will master tools and acquire skills equivalent to or perhaps greater than those of their teachers. And their knowledge of design and production positions them to be informed decision makers and co-publishers. The resulting changes in student roles and student/teacher relationships are welcomed by educators though they can seem threatening to some.

The effective use of tools and concepts by students is a primary objective of Consequential Learning and an important measure of its success. Every effort is made to involve all students in their application and, when necessary, to obtain the assistance of adults who are expert in using them. It is essential that teachers and mentors emphasize the value of effective application of tools and concepts so that students become aware of the new capacities they are gaining.

Collaboration. Consequential Learning projects position students to think and work together—to depend on each other—in order to achieve important outcomes subject to public judgment. Through the required collaboration, youngsters work with others and gain an appreciation of the benefits of joint effort, among them the development of character. As future entrepreneurs, employees, and managers, they must value cooperation and know how to collaborate, must understand how responsibility is apportioned, and must be prepared to assume leadership roles when necessary. Citizenship in a democracy involves more than casting individual votes. It requires a capacity and disposition for collaborative action aimed at shared goals, which are developed through experience working with others.

Documentation and Reflection. Students want records and other tangible evidence of their work. I realized how much they prize such materials when the PRSR was contacted by the family of a soldier serving in the first Gulf War. He had lost his copy of the anthology his high school class had published through the Awards Program in Writing and wanted another one sent to him as soon as possible. The request was consistent with what I have heard from other students involved in the program. Many have made it clear how much they and their families value the publications. After all, they are records of contributors' interests, capacities, and communities; and they are reminders of effective collaboration with classmates. The published collections had met the standards of a state university program and had been well-received by schools and communities. They documented students' learning as well as the efforts of their teachers.

In Consequential Learning projects, students produce outcomes that are records of their competence and interests. In an environment dominated by external evaluation, these projects provide contexts within which teachers and resource persons can help students make their own assessments of their capabilities. The growing emphasis on the development of metacognitive skills increases the need for youngsters to create, retain, and examine their work. It underscores the fact that awareness of oneself as a learner is indispensable to success in education and in life.

Public Demonstration of Knowledge and Understanding. Students are expected to demonstrate what they have learned in public settings. Standardized testing is a professionalized and centralized process that gives school constituencies and communities little, if any, opportunity for unmediated examination of student competence or for input regarding curriculum. All evidence of accountability is subsumed under the tests, and any other measure of public school performance is usually dismissed. This has not always been the case. David Mathews explains that, in the nineteenth century, schools held public examinations during which people could ask, see, and hear for themselves: "When schools had their students perform in public, as frequently happened, the community was the judge."[3] Consequential Learning programs provide school constituencies occasions for viewing and evaluating students' work. Three important benefits result from this practice, which supplements testing, increases adult expectations of students, and acknowledges that schools need an informed public response to their work.

First, the projects increase public support at a time when support for public education is declining. The current effort to alter public opinion and gain backing through standardized tests has not been and will not be successful. Although test results constitute easy currency for the media, education policy makers, and elected officials, their meaning is not clear. The results students achieve through Consequential Learning involve communities directly and position them to make their own assessments. They encourage participation of resource persons and other volunteers and of diverse local agencies and institutions.

I have heard teachers and principals complain that their communities will support athletics and the band but not academic work. There is no mystery here. Community members can see and assess sporting events and musical presentations. Extracurricular performances are well-established opportunities for "outsiders" to participate, whereas the academic life of schools remains basically hidden and is interpreted to them through letters and numbers that don't reveal enough. Products and performances that demonstrate academic accomplishment publicly are essential to public knowledge of what and how well schools are doing.

Second, the public presentations give students an audience that knows and cares about them. Teachers involved in PACERS writing and publishing projects have observed that things change when youngsters write for people with whom they are familiar. They report, for example, that students begin calling them at home to make sure that their work is correct, and they manifest a new willingness to re-write. As a student editor of a PCNP newspaper said to me: "I never thought much about a comma until I knew my grandmother would be reading this paper." The PCNP demonstrates that when students have consequential public tasks to carry out, the tools of the trade become relevant and valuable. It also confirms that students aspire to do good work for audiences composed of family members and others who will reinforce their efforts.

Third, public presentations of their works encourage students to move from memorizing of discrete pieces of information to demonstrating their understanding of them. "The facts, just the facts ma'am" may have been enough for Sergeant Friday; they are not sufficient for young people, who should be challenged to show that they know their significance. Of course, public demonstration of students' skills and of the results of their application also provides parents and community constituencies an opportunity to assess a project's significance for youngsters' development.

Authentic Learning Spaces

The characteristics of authentic learning spaces are essentially those identified by teachers, administrators, community members, and staff participating in planning and implementing the PACERS Rural Science Initiative. They have also been influenced by a variety of other PACERS initiatives and by the comments and judgments of students. An authentic learning space is authentic for all youngsters because it accommodates a variety of learning styles, allows for completion of multiple tasks, and displays the skills and accomplishments of every student.

Connection to Place. Authentic learning spaces are connected to the places where students live and are representative of the cultures with which they are identified. They help kids to understand their communities, which is especially important at a time when schools seem increasingly like franchises and where much of the construction and the "fare" are generic. As a result they appear to be local in the same way as a McDonald's. A youngster in Melbourne, Australia, told me she had moved several times from one high school to another and never had trouble finding classrooms, offices, or the loo because the school buildings were almost identical. But she added, "I never knew for sure where I was."

I was struck by the opposite and non-generic approach of a K-12 school in a small town in Washington State, which had broken out of the mold. Strongly influenced by the REAL entrepreneurship program, the school has made an effort to prepare students not only to think and act entrepreneurially but also to learn from and about their community. Elementary classrooms display street signs, mini-replicas of businesses and government offices, maps, pictures of individuals, and other indications of place. The high school features a variety of student-run businesses that provide needed local services and involve constant interaction between students and community members. There is no doubt about the school's locale, its interaction with the community, or the favorable impact of its place-related programs on student learning. The significance of place is indisputable, excluding its consideration from the educational process is detrimental to both schools and students.

Student Ownership and Responsibility. Authentic learning spaces are those in which students have meaningful responsibilities that create a sense of ownership. As a context for actions of immediate public consequence, they are real world situations where effective citizenship may be demonstrated. This notion was reinforced for me in the 1970s by the aspirations and efforts of members of the Student Coalition for Community Health and subsequently by a variety of projects involving youngsters of all ages. Those who initiated the SCCH confirmed that young people want to assume responsibility. They were determined to prove that they could make a difference in matters that count. An interview for positions on the SCCH's summer staff is illustrative. Two female applicants were asked a stock interview question: Why do you want to work? One said that she was tired of flipping burgers, the other that she was tired of working for a U.S. senator. They agreed, however, that boredom was not the only issue. Both very much wanted an opportunity to make decisions and to have significant responsibility for something that would make a difference. Although frying burgers in a fast-food joint and working in a senator's Washington office do not seem comparable, the two women shared a drive to take ownership, in effect, to assume the role of interested citizen.

Several outcomes of student ownership and responsibility should be emphasized. First, assuming responsibility for consequential public matters strengthens individual and civic character. Second, young people want such responsibility because they realize their good work changes adult attitudes toward them. It also influences youngster's self-images: they come to see themselves as capable of making a difference and of mastering the means to do so. Finally, taking responsibility for important work facilitates learning. Young people have a lot of grit; they deserve to be challenged by and to reap the rewards of demanding, consequential work.

Common Ground. Consequential Learning emphasizes creation of inclusive spaces and opportunities. In rural communities, many schools are still thought of as common ground. That notion is confirmed when school-related concerns prompt collaborative action or even when people gather for a football game. It is important to build on this understanding of the school as a public place. Consequential Learning projects provide intergenerational spaces that create or strengthen local ownership of schools. Such spaces promote learning as well as strong, informed community and constituency support.[4]

Cogency. Authentic learning spaces are compelling because they connect students to life (in aquaculture laboratories, for example) or the life of their communities. Educational settings often fail to do this. It is unlikely that many students would characterize their schools as lively. They should be able to do so.

Authentic learning spaces are immediately and transparently relevant. Former teacher John Harbuck described them as contexts in which "students don't have to put things off anymore." Reflecting on the aquaculture program at Florala High School in southern Alabama, he observed that, while the purpose of school seemed to be to prepare kids for the next grade, students working in the fishery were doing much more than just getting ready for the next grade or the next test. They had important jobs requiring the immediate application of knowledge. In order to keep the fish healthy, they had to operate as competent fish biologists. They were motivated to do so in part by their fear of discovering dead fish and in part by the prospect of successful fish harvests.

It is not very difficult to determine whether a learning environment is compelling for youngsters. Teachers and administrators involved in PACERS "living laboratories" projects point to students' strong desire to work in the labs as the obvious indication that these projects are interesting and relevant. Consequential Learning programs create environments in which kids not only see the immediate relevance of that they are learning but may also get a glimpse of their futures.

Context for Production. In authentic learning spaces, students are expected to generate public outcomes, so these settings contain tools (preferably industry standard) that enable them to be productive. PCNP offices, or classrooms, for example, are filled with computers, scanners, printers, telephones, cameras, software manuals, notepads, red pens, and address books. The activities pursued in authentic learning spaces are intended to create useful products. As is the case with almost everyone else, young people are interested in making things and are pleased when those things have value and are presented to a public audience.

Connections and Correlations

Consequential Learning approaches emphasize developing

and strengthening connections—especially those that tie schools to local communities, to resource persons and agencies, and to students' futures. They seek to identify correlations with external mandates and to provide means for professional collaboration within and among schools including cooperation that crosses grade levels and disciplines.

Local Communities. Consequential Learning projects seek to establish and strengthen connections between schools and local communities, including historical and ecological communities. (In the case of the latter, streams, watersheds, and the like become living laboratories as well as objects of study and documentation.) The focus on such connections underscores the centrality of place. It is also a means for affirming that local schools are public institutions and that local communities are significant learning resources and contexts.

External Mandates. Local interests and content are not high on the agendas of schools that follow standard curricula tailored to externally imposed standards. Failure to meet those standards is costly and can result in punitive action. Schools are in many respects like franchises, which must conform to priorities set by the head office. In some instances, the outside control configures school life extensively, through scripted curricula and detailed orders regarding when and how required content must be "served up." It is necessary to bear in mind that all projects must be correlated with external mandates and must measure up to standards established by boards and specified in policies that fail to acknowledge differences among, and recognize the importance of, local knowledge, or to value appropriately the contributions of local teachers.

Establishing the connections and correlations with external requirements can be difficult, however, and not always for the reasons most likely to be cited. Consequential Learning projects provide strong evidence that they more than accommodate external rules and regulations. But that evidence may not be enough to prompt action on the part of educators disposed to remain inside the box. Teachers and administrators recognize that a "franchised" system ostensibly values conformity and promotes the use of standard procedures to achieve standard goals. Franchised approaches can be beneficial, especially if the products are burgers or rental movies. But young people are not inanimate units; their schools are located in particular places and those places influence their interests and performance. Place-related learning is motivating and relevant for students. It helps them fulfill external requirements and a great deal more.

Resource Persons and Agencies. Professionals, post-secondary institutions, and businesses stand ready to assist schools. Why aren't they doing so? Perhaps it is because you can't do anything if there isn't anything for you to do, as Yogi Berra might put it. The fact is that help follows when invitations are accompanied by clear directions and cogent statements of purposes.

The approach taken by the reading program of a small rural Alabama elementary school that succeeded in acquiring the assistance of parents demonstrates how this can work. The school is located in a poor community, where people have difficulty getting around and taking time off from work. In addition many of the students' parents were themselves very young and in need of assistance. The program insured that parents received weekly "assignments," which explained in straightforward language what they were to do to help their children and why. Each week parents completed forms documenting what they had done, and they met twice annually with teachers to review their youngsters' work. A parents' party was held at the end of the school year to celebrate their children's progress.

The formula was a simple one. Teachers began with the view that individuals outside the school were needed to help students learn. In this case they were parents, but in other settings they might be resource persons or agencies. Having decided that others should be involved in their students' education, the teachers issued an invitation that clarified goals and specified how parents could help. The assignments communicated to parents what was at stake and what was needed to ensure that the children learned to read. Students' reading improved, parents became involved in the life of the school, and teachers received more satisfaction from their work.

The culture of schools does not tend to promote interaction with non-educators. Parents are often criticized for their failure to help, but the negative judgment seems rarely to be accompanied by suggestions for making effective use of their time. Consequential Learning holds that the education of youngsters should involve people who are not professional educators. Individuals and agencies are willing to help, and well-defined requests for assistance will elicit strong support. In *Bowling Alone*, Robert Putnam cites the finding of Yale psychiatrist James Comer that "parental participation can improve school performance . . . but only if parents are given real decision-making responsibility and are placed in positions suited to their knowledge and skills."[5]

Consequential Learning projects find and make use of valuable external resources and capacities beyond those offered by parents. People and agencies are ready to help but they can't do anything, if they don't know what is needed.

Students' Futures. Consequential Learning connects young people to their futures. Students work with professionals, who teach them to use the tools and concepts of their professions. These practitioners become mentors and links to post-secondary opportunities. And the real world nature of the projects gives students an invaluable preview of work options, a look that many young people do not have.

The linking of young people to future options is especially crucial with the majority of schools with which I have worked because they serve a high percentage of students in poverty and with more limited connections. Their rural communities have been devastated by outmigration and the closure of a variety of institutions and businesses. For example, a teacher, explaining the difference community population decline had made in his school, identified as a very significant factor the loss of students whose parents were professionals and who had gone to college. As a student in the school twenty-five years earlier his classmates included the sons and daughters of doctors and lawyers. From them he had himself made connections to college and ultimately to teaching. Now he noted those links and models were gone. He concluded that it was difficult to replace them with information on careers that students did not see connected to people whom they knew. Obviously outsiders are needed to fill the gap.

Complex Teacher Responsibilities

There is nothing new in the notion that teaching is demanding. Consequential Learning projects ask teachers to take on a number of responsibilities that go beyond what is required by conventional classroom work. Some teachers say the projects have provided them their first opportunities to do what they had hoped to do on entering the profession. In other words the roles were those of a professional.

Coordination. Teachers are responsible for project coordination, which requires them to organize, plan, recruit people and resources, implement, and evaluate. As coordinators, teachers must foster collaboration and help clarify responsibilities of students and other participants. I have often asked youngsters to describe the differences between their experience in standard classrooms and their experience in PACERS projects. One student, whose class was writing a community history, responded with two graphics. First, she drew a large black dot at the top of a page. Below that, she drew many significantly smaller ones, connecting them to the large dot with straight lines. The student explained that the drawing represented her classroom before the project was introduced. In the second drawing, a dot in the center of the page was surrounded by slightly smaller dots. Some lines ran connected the smaller dots directly, others ran from smaller dots to the larger one or though it to other smaller dots. Commenting on the second drawing, the student observed simply that the teacher now helped them to work together.

Curriculum Development. Teaching is an art as well as a profession, and its practitioners are therefore expected to be creative. Teaching is not simply following a script or text or drilling for tests before a test—both of which good teachers consider boring and irrelevant. No class room instruction is more effective than that which is informed by teachers' interests and creativity.

Teachers involved in Consequential Learning projects have developed new instructional strategies, written new curricula, and designed new learning spaces. And teachers directing similar projects in PACERS routinely assist with planning and implementing related professional development programs. Once again, I should point out that the prevailing educational culture tends toward passivity. Consequential Learning calls for initiative and creativity, and both teachers and students demonstrate that they prosper under such expectations.

Learning. Consequential Learning projects are challenging

and require that teachers add to their knowledge of subject matter, reflect on and strengthen their practice, and find out about the needs and resources of their communities. Teachers are energized by opportunities to learn, and in the process of learning they become models for their students. Projects should be evaluated in part by their ability to assist teachers to grow in their practice and content knowledge.

Collegiality. Consequential Learning tends to strengthen collegial relationships within schools and to create such relationships between teachers and persons outside the school. Larry Long, the founder of Elders' Wisdom and Children's Song, explains that, in the process of song writing and recitation preparation, teachers and students share ideas about both content and form. They make collaborative decisions; and, according to Long, the process often results in increased mutual respect. Collegiality is a given in demanding projects like those involving the publication of a community newspaper or operation of a fishery. Although teachers direct the projects and have the ultimate authority over them, the complex requirements of Consequential Learning initiatives compel them to establish collegial relationships with students in order to sustain the work.

Collegial ties to students are pluses for teachers; also valuable are the associations teachers develop with the resource persons they recruit to assist with the projects. The "experts" are there to help achieve important public results, not to give lectures and then leave. Their stake in the project prompts them to collaborate and they become the teachers' colleagues and allies.

Assessment and Interpretation. These days teachers are increasingly being assessed and decreasingly making assessments. It is important for both their profession and individual teachers that they exercise and improve their assessment skills. Many

Consequential Learning projects suggest new ways for teachers to understand student learning and call for their professional interpretation of processes and outcomes. Project sustainability depends on teachers' judgment of how external mandates can be met and how projects create and realize more challenging and complex expectations.

The outcomes of Consequential Learning projects offer local communities and school constituencies a basis for evaluating teacher capacity. Teachers benefit from the opportunity that the public work of their students gives them to clarify their professional objectives and demonstrate their competence.

Enjoyment

Consequential Learning projects are meant to be enjoyable to participating students. Those who organized the Student Coalition for Community Health intended to find their work satisfying; in fact, they decided that enjoyment would be one criterion for determining the success of their summer health fairs. In a very demanding work environment where high stakes outcomes were being sought and responsibilities were weighty and public, having fun was not a given for them. However, both students and professional evaluators judged that the experience had, in fact, been enjoyable and that the enjoyment was rooted in collaborative work that had challenged participants, allowed them to demonstrate their personal capacity and commitment, and connected them to a variety of community members, professionals, and places.

Over time, I have heard both sides of the story about fun and schools. On one occasion, a PACERS project was canceled because it was "fun" and, therefore considered incompatible with serious work. The cancellation reflects lurking fear that somewhere, somehow students may enjoy learning. But many educators rightly insist that challenging work can and should be a source of personal satisfaction for young people, and they make it their business to ensure that students attain that.

Principles

Young people are members of communities, and they have privileges and responsibilities that derive from their citizenship. They are competent, interested in life, and moving quickly toward futures beyond school. Consequential Learning principles are coordinates for planning approaches and activities that take these characteristic seriously. They call for the creation of educational opportunities that are challenging, connected to place, active, and entrepreneurial, opportunities that allow students to behave as citizens and to produce outcomes that they understand to be important for their learning, their self-awareness, and their futures, as well as for communities.

Consequential Learning values the professionalism of teachers and calls for their creativity. It places them in public contexts where they can acquire new resources and establish new connections for their students, demonstrate their competence, and fashion new alliances between schools and their constituencies. Consequential Learning also recognizes that schools are public institutions that need and deserve the contributions of individuals with skills, means, and clout essential for implementing challenging educational programs.

Section 3

Consequential Learning in Action

Consequential Learning's guiding principles have been derived from the work of many individuals, schools, and organizations. I have chosen to focus on three long-term efforts that embody these principles particularly well and that demonstrate the results of their application: the PACERS Community Newspaper Project (PCNP), Elders' Wisdom and Children's Song (EWCS), and the aquaculture programs at Florala High School and Loachapoka Elementary School in rural Alabama. I have worked closely with all three programs, I am familiar with their successes and failures, and I have been privileged to watch them mature over a decade or more. I am indebted to teachers, administrators, community members, and resource persons associated with these ventures for sharing their observations, documentation of the projects and for doing the work necessary to make them effective. Resource materials relating to the programs are readily available—guidebooks, sample curricula, and examples of program outcomes that greatly expand on what is presented here. Teachers and other professionals who have taken leadership roles in these efforts welcome the opportunity to share their perspectives with schools and communities interested in undertaking similar work.

The programs have all received national recognition, and they have either been replicated or have directly influenced similar initiatives in several states. Adaptable to local situations, they reveal and call upon local resources. They provide lively, effective learning contexts for a broad range of youngsters because they accommodate a variety of learning styles and interests. In all of them, students and teachers become active learners, use critical judgment, and produce outcomes that are significant to themselves and to the places where they live.

The programs have been resilient and have prospered, in some cases against significant odds. They call forth the leadership of individuals committed to improving their schools and communities, and they connect learning and place in ways that promote young people's citizenship and community membership and that afford opportunities to see themselves as persons who can make a difference.

PACERS Community Newspaper Project

Established collaboratively in the early 1990s by a few member schools in the PACERS Cooperative and the Program for Rural Services and Research, the PCNP has involved more than thirty schools and many hundreds of students in rural Alabama and has served as a model for other schools and communities in the United States, Australia, and Canada.

The idea of student-published community newspapers was proposed to PRSR staff by Kathy Clancy in the early 1990s when she was director of student media at the University of Alabama. Her suggestions were well received and coincided with nascent PRSR considerations of school-based media. As a professional working directly with university students, she was in a position to help establish early parameters for the project and to reinforce her contention that youngsters could meet the challenge of publishing newspapers. Clancy was one of many journalists and journalism students to contribute to the PCNP, and she early maintained that the involvement of professionals was essential if the project was to succeed. Journalists, regional and statewide newspapers, media organizations, and university faculty have readily assisted in the effort. As is often suggested, this kind of specific, project-based linking of schools and students to outside professionals is crucial for the success of projects, for augmenting school resources, and for connecting young people to their futures.

During the planning stages of the PACERS Better Schools Program, several high schools decided to undertake the PCNP. Only one of them had ever published a student paper; and it would prove quite a stretch for that school to move to the production of what would become a commercially successful local newspaper. The project obviously required a substantial commitment on the part of all the participating schools. Their students and teachers proved to be up to the task; and, under the leadership of Jim Wrye, PRSR staff member and PCNP coordinator, they developed high standards. Their rigorous planning, training, and evaluation paved the way for many schools to join the PCNP. The collaboration among the schools was a kind of buddy system for beginning publishers, with participants helping each other to stay afloat. It was an early lesson in the benefits of such collaboration—among schools as well as between schools and outside agencies and resource persons. It also became clear that this kind of collaboration requires a good deal of nurturing to become a standard mode of operation.

It is obviously not a good idea to begin a demanding, school-based project that cannot get the nod from students. Many of those attending small rural high schools across Alabama have demonstrated substantial interest in the PCNP. They seem to be motivated to assist their communities, to demonstrate their competence and concern, and to learn new skills in lively classroom and extracurricular settings.

At the turn of the twentieth century there were about a thousand commercial newspapers in Alabama; during the ensuing hundred years, 90 percent of them folded operation. Among the communities that lost local media, those in rural Alabama were the front-runners. High school students who helped fashion the PCNP weren't familiar with the statistics, but they knew the consequences of the losses. A tenth grader from a northern Alabama coal mining community said that he wanted students in his school to publish a local paper because it is not possible to have a community without means to share information. In a matter-of-fact aside, he added that democracies, too, depend on the free access of information and ideas. It was a strong expression of the students' awareness of themselves as citizens and members of communities.

Students discovered evidence of defunct nineteenth-century newspapers in several communities which were subsequently unearthed in courthouse basements and other storage spots. They obtained permission and made arrangements to use the original names for their new publications. The re-establishment of the dead papers is a metaphor for the capacity of schools and students to revitalize and support community life.

In a PCNP planning session, a student from the Pine Belt of southwestern Alabama wanted to publish a newspaper in order to give his community a voice.[1] Other students agreed when he added that only death and destruction in their community garnered coverage in countywide newspapers. The youngster later told me that he was himself something like his community: he had a speech impediment and knew that writing would be an important means for self-expression; the proposed paper might fill the same function for his town. The student observations reported here and elsewhere in this book are, in my view, both sophisticated and insightful. Representatives of foundations, resource persons, and other adults reviewing projects and meeting with students have had a similar impression of their comments. I am not saying that the projects give students insight; I am convinced, however, that they provide important contexts within which students can reflect on and express their values and aspirations.

The comments and opinions of young people in schools across rural Alabama guided planning of the PCNP. They were usually the first to recognize the promise of the project as a means for making a difference in the places where they lived. Young people involved in the planning understood the potential of agencies of mass communication and expressed their own interest in the media. In conversations about community newspapers, students mentioned the possibility of radio stations and the production of video material for area television stations. Their interest was not unique among young people as indicated by the many examples in the US and other countries of students operating media of various sorts.[2]

Students felt that, by publishing newspapers, they could help their communities understand young people and communicate their own capacities and concerns. It is clear that they aspired to the status of community members and wanted to shelve the stereotypes that too often separate them from older generations.

These young people correctly anticipated that a relevant and new technology experience was in the offing. Computers and software were essential to the trade, and kids were eager to master the skills they required. Indeed, curricular and extracurricular options related to computing were extremely attractive to students.

Publishing a newspaper is obviously an exacting task for young people, even given the support and training provided by teachers and other professionals. The students who produced the first PCNP papers knew they were taking on a difficult assignment. They did not have the experience and skills—including those related to decision making, problem solving and collaboration—that would be needed. Reporting, designing, selling ads, establishing and following editorial policies, managing staff, and other complex and often unanticipated tasks presented themselves to the aspiring publishers. To do the job well would require students to learn a great deal. Even with papers up and running, new students—sometimes called rookies—must be trained as staff members graduate. The need for developing skills and for inculcating high publication standards remains constant.

Students are expected to do the work of professional journalists. There are, of course, differences between a school-based newspaper and a commercial enterprise. Administrators and teachers have responsibilities and authority that must on occasion be exercised and that may set aside student work and judgments. Nonetheless, the papers are published by students using the tools and practices of journalists. They make crucial decisions regarding both content and design, and adults looking at PACERS papers for the first time observe that the publications are of professional quality and are surprised that they are student-published. The fact is that expectations of young people are not high enough nor is there generally an adequate recognition of their commitment and competence. By the lights of the PCNP, instructional challenges to students are often too mechanical, too simplistic, and too limited.

Consequential Learning is not intended to serve a select group of students; it seeks to foster opportunities for all youngsters. The PCNP has involved a large and diverse group of students, all of them active participants in the production of the newspapers.

A survey revealed that staffs for the papers during the initial five years of the project were composed primarily of females and members of minority groups. This breakdown was not expected, partly because so much of the work involved the use of computers. Prevailing statistics on computer education and application do not suggest that female students are likely to be a majority in a program with strong technology components. Also, since the total population of the participating schools were not 50 percent minority, the data revealed the project's appeal for these youngsters. My experience with the PCNP is that females and minorities are not only drawn to the project, they prosper in it.

A handful of kids may take the lead in the publication of a particular school's paper, but the work requires the contributions of all. The tasks are varied and time constraints are pressing. It is, therefore, clear that continuing publication of the newspapers is testimony to broad and effective student involvement. Moreover, the papers serve as vehicles for the writing of youngsters who are not on the PCNP staff. Some project advisors make all the students in their classes "reporters," requiring them to prepare articles suitable for the paper (though not all of them are actually published). In the case where this was done most comprehensively, students' writing assessment scores improved immediately. Some PCNP papers have elementary school sections devoted to the writings and drawings of younger kids, thereby providing them a community audience and further expanding schools' local connections.

The project's ability to engage students across grades and to address a variety of subjects increases its value to schools. The newspapers create opportunities for student mentoring, for interdisciplinary learning, and for connecting writing to real audiences. And their impact has been schoolwide. The PCNP obviously constitutes an attractive curricular and/or extracurricular option; but first study of the publications' influence revealed that they had increased the student body's sense of positive relations between the school and the community. The newspapers are the public work of students and are important links between schools and communities. So, it is not surprising that they have fostered stronger relationships.

Publishing a paper is a complex enterprise calling for a variety of skills: writing, designing, selling, interviewing, and managing. The breadth of the requirements creates opportunities for students whose motivations, capacities, and learning styles differ widely. As a result, the project attracts and serves well many students who do not prosper within standard classroom instructional and evaluation formats. They do well with PCNP work because they have an opportunity to use their talents and their own ways of learning. In addition, students are challenged by the diverse roles and responsibilities that come with participation on the newspaper staffs. They speak candidly about their strengths, weaknesses, and personal development in relation to the demands of their staff assignments. The PCNP offers students a crucial opportunity for self-assessment.

Teachers and students in the project routinely talk about its capacity to motivate and even to cause youngsters to remain in school. Being able to show competence is obviously a factor in students' increased interest in learning and in their willingness to stay. Students are also encouraged by the way that the project helps them to see into and make connections with their futures.

As is the case with the other exemplary programs, the PCNP produces outcomes that benefit a variety of constituencies, beginning with students—those who are on the newspaper staff or who are part-time contributors as well as the larger student population. Benefits to students overlap with benefits to teachers as they jointly try to realize common goals. I have seen them working together with the devotion and camaraderie that signify a community of learning. The newspapers also connect students and teachers engaged in the project to local communities. Although the benefits are discussed below under three rubrics, it is important to stress that no outcome is more significant than the development of intergenerational relationships and effective connections between schools and communities.

Students. Participation in the PCNP gives students a chance to improve their reading and writing skills; to master complex computer technology; and to practice gathering, analyzing, and presenting information; to develop self-esteem; to learn to meet deadlines; and to explore career paths and gain perspective on the relationship between school and their future lives. Yet administrators are occasionally unwilling or unable to recognize that publishing newspapers constitutes a very effective learning experience. They may fail to see this because PCNP work and the benefits derived from it do not conform to the traditional models of classes, test taking, and passive education culture. The fact is that the project and its outcomes are tied as much to the standards of the information age as to those of the industrial age, though the latter seems dominant in American education. They also relate more to the real world than do the majority of school programs.

Students participating in the PCNP carry out responsibilities of citizenship and of membership in communities. They learn about the places where they live, and they learn what it means to accept and fulfill obligations those places impose. And they learn to do these things with each other. The experience contributes significantly to their personal and civic character formation.

The project helps youngsters make connections to their futures. This is especially important, since the work attracts many students who are not considered "likely to succeed." Journalism is the most obvious career path opened by the PCNP. Students do the work of journalists, they meet journalists and journalism teachers, and they receive training that is comparable to post-secondary school journalism instruction. Many PCNP students become stringers for larger newspapers, further extending their experience with reporting. Publishing a paper, however, opens up other possibilities—in information technology, graphics and design, business, and public relations, among others. The project also helps young people gain the confidence and experience necessary for an active and self-determined pursuit of any future. The core skills of gathering, sorting, and sharing information—the upshot of working on newspapers—are, of course, essential.

PCNP newspapers are businesses which create and distribute products and sell services. Staff members deal with the public and with other businesses; money changes hands and must be accounted for and invested. Business plans are important tools for the papers and several good ones, along with processes for their preparation, have been developed and followed.[3] Preparing for success in a participatory economy is essential for all young people, including those who are underrepresented and least likely to enjoy entrepreneurial opportunities. The PCNP is a model context in which students can become actively engaged in the economy. Young people often find it difficult to believe that their work has value. The problem is exemplified by the initial reluctance of some PCNP students to sell ads. Thanks to the adults who helped them understand the worth of their product, newspaper staffers have become good salespersons, garnering considerable revenue for their publications. It is a long way from the typical student experience of selling candy for school projects to selling a service that contributes to the purchasers' commercial success.

Teachers. Teachers directing the projects described here and others with which I have worked have had many opportunities to come together to reflect on their efforts. In addition to hearing assessments of the newspaper advisers in collegial and professional development settings, I have interviewed many of them in depth and have read their written evaluations. Teachers' takes on the project are always realistic; they call attention to the need for more time, stronger administrative support, access to the next generation of computer technology, and incorporation of the project into the formal curriculum.

Despite a number of challenges, the PCNP teachers I have talked to generally regard this very demanding project as both viable and worthwhile. They are highly motivated and have demonstrated a capacity and willingness to solve problems. If that were not the case, there would not be a PCNP. These educators view the newspapers as unique contexts for teaching basic academic skills, for engaging and motivating a broad range of students, for opening up future possibilities to them, for keeping some youngsters from leaving school and for giving some an opportunity to succeed in school for the first time. Underscoring the character-forming aspects of the work, teachers also note that publishing a newspaper requires that students fulfill meaningful individual and collaborative responsibilities in a timely fashion. The PCNP is very compatible with the professional goals and personal aspirations of teachers, making them enthusiastic project advocates.

The work affords teachers new professional associations and new relationships with the local community. The gratitude of community members and meaningful exchanges with colleagues contribute significantly to both their motivation and their professional growth.

Communities. The student-published newspapers contain pertinent local information and record local history, reporting on the births, marriages, celebrations, and deaths of community members as well as other local matters. Business is stimulated through advertisements and stories, and on occasion PCNP participants receive word from a local enterprise that newspaper coverage has kept them afloat. The papers' revenues tend to rise during election seasons as candidates purchase space. The newspapers are means for sharing information on important questions affecting community well-being. The location of pipelines and quarries, with potential impact on safety and the environment, exemplifies the kind of issues the newspapers cover in a manner that enables communities to determine and protect their best interests. Town council and school board meetings are routinely reported on, as are locally relevant actions of the state board of education and the legislature.

The PCNP papers are generally the only media show in town. As such, they fill an information gap; and, in so doing, they meet a serious community need. The newspapers are excellent examples of community journalism. Their value is widely recognized, and they attract substantial local interest. I once asked a principal about the status of his school's PCNP. He replied that all was going well except that he was being bombarded with phone calls and people were stopping him in town to ask when the next edition would be out; if the paper was late, the phone lines became a little overheated. Similarly, students in one school have spoken about the enthusiastic responses to their paper, especially at the senior center. The interest and commendation of local elders is an important outcome, and the newspapers serve as "visas" permitting the youngsters to cross the generational border.

In sum, there is a lot at stake in the publication of PCNP papers. By bridging the gap between schools and communities and between the generations, and at the same time enhancing local identity, they provide an essential service for their communities or neighborhoods. They make clear that youngsters are smarter than previously assumed and that they are interested in serving their communities and able to do so. Teachers involved in the PCNP demonstrate their own competence and see their students grow personally and academically. The kids become more mature in defining and meeting their responsibilities. Perhaps most important, the project provides answers to long-standing questions about the nature and purposes of educational institutions. Schools become creators and dispensers of information as well as demonstrators of technologies central to the information economy. They become places where students can fulfill the responsibilities of citizenship through consequential work that includes making school life more transparent and more accessible to the publics the schools are intended to serve. Through the PCNP, schools make clear that they appreciate the assistance of outside professionals, from whom students learn and though whom they make connections to their futures.

Elders' Wisdom and Children's Song

Created by troubadour and community organizer Larry Long, EWCS is a one-week program in which elders go into elementary schools and tell their life stories to children who then prepare recitations and songs about what they have heard; these are later performed at community-wide celebrations. Before describing the program in more detail, there are several of its characteristics that are important to set out. Students have fun in their classrooms while learning how to carry out an important public task; the work is arts based; nonprofessional seniors spend time in the classrooms and their lives are the subject of study. EWCS activities often cross disciplinary lines; teachers go beyond standard scripts and invent new opportunities and strategies for learning and self-expression in the process; and, in a role-expanding approach, they share decision-making responsibilities with their students. Community members, attending the public celebrations in large numbers, observe students sing and read their compositions and are then able to make their own judgments about the capacities of both kids and teachers. One teacher said the celebration was "language arts in full view." In addition, Long explains that children are expected to "show love to the elders," and participating teachers and administrators often use the word "love" to describe students' interactions with the seniors. These characteristics emphasize—sometimes against the opposite perspective—that effective schooling can be fun; that parents and other outsiders can and will contribute to kids' learning; that such programs as EWCS help get kids ready to do better on the tests; that the study of communities and elders is of great interest to children; that teachers and kids, through the arts, can create materials and undertake performances that enhance the most basic skills that should be honed in students.

Several years ago, Ruth Davis, an elementary principal in a PACERS school, had scheduled the weeklong EWCS residency that ends with a public celebration of the lives of elders and of the community at large. Davis and her teachers were well-prepared for the work. Then she and her faculty were struck by the celebration's proximity to test-taking season, which seemed too close for comfort. Davis thought that perhaps the program should be cancelled; after all, her school serves students who are by and large the children of poverty in Alabama's Black Belt—they are plenty smart, but less likely than the children of wealth and privilege to succeed on the tests. But, the die had been cast, the money raised, and the commitments made. The EWCS celebration and residency proceeded on schedule, producing a surprise benefit: the children were more motivated and more enthusiastic about school, even tests, than they ever had been before. They were, Davis commented "ready for anything." The celebration had evidently energized students and given the school a new sense of capacity and purpose—developments that have been experienced by EWCS programs in many other schools.

The EWCS process has been successfully implemented in a variety of communities, rural and urban, throughout the United States. What does it accomplish? How do its approaches and outcomes reflect the premises and goals of Consequential Learning? Again, the benefits overlap the categories in which they are presented, in part because the roles of participants are not circumscribed by the usual boundaries. For example, both teachers and students become learners and decision makers, elders become teachers and de facto textbooks, and the community becomes the school house. A final section describes the effect of EWCS documentation on local communities and beyond.

Students. Bonnie Jean Flom, former principal of Neurstrand Elementary School in Minnesota, explained that her staff's primary objective was to involve every student in EWCS programs, an objective that has proved attainable throughout the intitution's six-year experience with EWCS. All students listen, write, and sing; all help decide on the content of songs and recitations; and all come to know the elders and work with Long and local musicians participating in the project. At the performance, some students read from the recitations, some welcome community members and present roses to the elders, and some help with the sound system or with the stage set. Because EWCS affords a variety of opportunities for students and calls upon a diversity of skills, the project is able to accommodate the goal of many teachers and administrators to involve every child.

Participating students work with each other, and they also work with adults—Long and other assisting musicians and songwriters, teachers, and local elders. Youngsters begin as learners and are prepared by adults for listening, writing, decision making, and performing. Their relationships with these adults can be very collegial. For example, students are fully involved in the process of composing recitations and songs, and in many cases, their ideas will supersede suggestions by Long and their teachers. Obviously, when adults take students seriously in a meaningful intergenerational setting, they are encouraged to think of themselves as decision makers, whose views are worthy of consideration.

Listening is a crucial responsibility of students in EWCS, and one they eagerly accept. Kids listen intently to elders because their stories are engaging and because the youngsters are responsible for fashioning the spoken narratives into recitations and songs. The process is very different from what might be called "tape recorder listening"—that is, listening solely in order to retain information at least until the test. Critical listening for the purpose of making decisions and taking action is a skill that must be mastered by all who are preparing to be citizens in a democracy.

EWCS supports young people's personal and civic character

formation because it is a program in which they have consequential responsibilities. They are asked to honor, reflect on, and portray the lives of elders in public settings. It is no small matter to be challenged to listen carefully, to record thoughts accurately, and to pitch in with others to select and arrange the words that are going to tell the story of another person's life. Students of all ages are quick to assume these responsibilities, moreover the EWCS process offers kids many opportunities to take initiative in moving beyond the "assignments." In Goodsprings, Alabama, for example, two students, entirely on their own, went to the home of a senior who for health reasons could not meet with the class. Intent on hearing and sharing the man's story and armed with their own tape recorder and notebooks, they conducted an extensive interview. While the quality of their work was excellent (it was the basis for a song included on a Smithsonian recording) the real story was the youngsters' ownership of the project. In Consequential Learning, it is crucial that students hold title to their work.

Hank Fridell, principal of East Elementary School in Spearfish, South Dakota, suggests that kids are often disconnected from their communities and wonders whether they sometimes feel as if society wants them to "disappear." I have heard similar language from students and teachers in a variety of places. According to Fridell, EWCS is a powerful means for young people to reverse the disconnect. Participants are seen as doing good work that strengthens their communities. But Fridell points to an even more important consequence: EWCS "lets kids know what kind of power they can have to make a difference." During the performance they see the positive emotional response of elders and hear the applause of other community members, signals that they have done well and made things better for the seniors. Personal confidence and awareness of having the ability to make a difference are essential underpinnings of active citizenship, or effective membership, and welcome products of EWCS.

Of course, the stories of elders themselves are instructive. Seniors involved in the process take their responsibilities very seriously; they choose their words carefully and seldom moralize. As indicated by their roles, elders participate not to tell young people how to live but to tell them about how they have lived. Consequently, students hear life stories emphasizing such themes as hard work and hard times, courage and aspiration, appreciation of and responsibility to others, injustice and efforts to make things right, family and fun. They then sort through what they have heard, extracting what they find most interesting; in other words, kids are positioned to reflect on the narratives of persons whose lives are considered exemplary. And their reflections help them to think about their own lives and become more self-conscious about the communities in which they live.

Elders know that kids are honoring them, and their involvement in EWCS is often a high point of their lives, with powerful implications for them and their families. Seniors make clear their gratitude to the young people to whom they entrust their stories and who are serving as their biographers. The benefits of this esteem-building affirmation of the participating elders are compounded by the thanks and admiration students receive from elders' families and other community members who attend the celebrations. Participating youngsters know and are proud that they are making a difference for the seniors and for their communities.

Children enjoy taking part in a creative process and in a public performance. As Long observes: "They like to see their words go on a board and in a booklet and hear them repeated and sung." Fridell reports that he hears students singing songs they helped to write years after their performance. Kids are also able to keep written as well as audio and video records of their work. Not unlike letters awarded for athletic excellence, the products of EWCS include meaningful tokens of youngsters' efforts and achievements in very challenging circumstances.

Many participating students and elders establish lasting relationships with each other. Teachers and administrators involved in EWCS point to its ability to connect kids and seniors in ways that transcend the program and even the school.

Teachers. Many teachers have said, during evaluation and reflection sessions, that EWCS is the best thing that ever happened at their schools. They value EWCS because it is a context in which students can be creative. Teachers point with dismay to the diminishing opportunities in schools for children to engage in creative activity. They understand that artistic expression and experience are vital to their students' lives, and they relish the chance to help youngsters accomplish important goals by means of the arts. Although they state it less forcefully, teachers value their own opportunities to participate in a creative process. They are pleased to be helping kids write the songs and personal histories, which themselves become useful instructional materials. EWCS may also prompt teachers to develop additional activities involving community history and the arts.

As a result of EWCS, teachers are known and honored by their communities, and they learn more about the places where they teach. They are seen as facilitators of children's good work and as contributors to community well-being. And they sometimes develop relationships with participating elders who later become volunteers and support the work of their schools.

Schools. EWCS bridges the gap between schools and communities, bringing them together in unique ways. Some participants report that the program brought the community into the life of their schools for the first time in memory. Through the EWCS process, schools honor and record the lives of community elders, serve as places for community-wide celebrations; and create means for ongoing involvement of community members with their work.

The program often generated new instructional strategies. The EWCS approach can be used for teaching a variety of subjects—social studies is an obvious example. A school nurse explained that the process had prompted her to have health professionals tell students stories related to their career choices and their work. And a principal reported that she had arranged for kids to interview and learn from seniors serving as resource persons for her school's greenhouse and gardening project.

Communities. EWCS bridges the gap between schools and communities in ways that confer honor on community members and that celebrate and affirm local life. Community responses bring home the significance of both the process and the concluding event. Teachers frequently report that EWCS celebrations attract the largest audiences they have ever seen at their schools. Why is this so? People come to see their children and grandchildren perform, and friends of the elders being honored come to pay their respects. Also, some community members simply like to spend time in their schools, and EWCS gives them a good reason to do so.

Documentation and Community History. Teachers and administrators planning the PACERS Better Schools' projects manifested a good deal of interest in engaging students in work documenting their communities' past. Oral and photographic histories were prepared, community history classes were offered, and local history sections of PACERS newspapers were published and widely distributed. All of this was evidence that students could function as local historians and produce high-quality work, in the process expanding the role of schools and defining them more clearly as community institutions that generate important local information.

In PACERS schools and other settings, EWCS demonstrates the capacity of students to recover and record local history. By telling the life stories of seniors in recitation and song, participants the EWCS process honors community members and confirm that "we all make history every day," to quote one Alabamian. Smithsonian Folkways formed a partnership with PACERS, the PRSR, and Larry Long to produce *Here I Stand,* a recorded collection of EWCS stories and songs featuring elders and children from rural Alabama. The Smithsonian CD and other CDs, as well as audio and video tapes of EWCS interviews and celebrations, have been distributed widely, testifying to the strong interest of families and communities in the documentation the project provides.

The EWCS process occasionally uncovers extraordinary stories with national implications communities may have forgotten. Larry Long's early implementation of the process in Okema, Oklahoma, helped bring Woody Guthrie, a native son, more fully into the life and memory of his community. In Beatrice, Alabama elementary school students listened to Ezra Cunningham tell of his groundbreaking civil rights work. Although familiar to many local adults, Cunningham's life and wisdom were basically unknown to community youngsters; and, prior to the EWCS event, there was little written or recorded information about his life. Clarence Hupka survived the sinking of the USS *Indianapolis* and told his story to Nebraska children. The song, written collaboratively by Long and the class that heard him, was so powerful that the students were invited to sing it at the annual meeting of the *Indianapolis* survivors. Buck Barber, a Native American, worked and performed with children who had sung his life's song at an EWCS celebration, eventually taking them to the boarding school he had been forced to attend. And Gladys Milton, a mid-wife whose work had benefited thousands in rural areas near the Alabama/Florida border, was portrayed by students in an EWCS celebration as a virtual saint.

These kinds of stories give perspective to students learning about their communities and their country, and the students in turn give their communities a powerful record of people and place.

Florala and Loachapoka Aquaculture Programs

As its name suggests, Florala, Alabama sits on the border between Alabama and Florida. It is typical of many rural communities in the state. Florala is not affluent; it has been negatively affected by rural out-migration, one of the consequences of limited local opportunity. Its high school serves a large number of students eligible for free or reduced-cost lunches; and, as is the case with many rural schools, it prepares young people to leave the community. It is more difficult to equip them to stay, which is the other part of the twofold challenge facing rural schools. More than a decade ago, John Harbuck, who was the high school's vocational-agriculture teacher, began, in collaboration with PACERS and the PRSR, to realize a long-term dream of setting up a fishery and initiating a comprehensive aquaculture program. He was convinced that these would offer students an effective context for learning science and preparing for good jobs. Harbuck hoped that the school could find support for establishing the program and for eventually equipping a state-of-the-art facility.

With assistance from the PACERS Cooperative, Harbuck was able to setup a small aquaculture unit. The initial effort was well-received by students and adult members of the community, who were open to the possibility of building a more elaborate facility. The program's early success and its bold plans generated additional contributions of time, funds, and expertise. Members of the area's legislative delegation visited, were impressed, and provided support for the expansion. A state-of-the-art aquaculture unit was the result. Community members were proud of the new facility and of the interest it commanded; it was accessible to them, and they felt ownership of it.

Area fish farmers came to share and gain information, and postsecondary institutional reps and employers came to assist and recruit. For youngsters participating in the program, the opportunity to work with aquaculture professionals proved invaluable. Harbuck reports that an extension agent, stationed about seventy-five miles from Florala, visited frequently and that students were always eager to see him; they peppered him with questions and talked to him as though he were a close friend. The Christmas card members of the class members sent the agent was signed, "From your students."

As word of the operation spread, people from across the state and then the region began to arrive in Florala to investigate what was rapidly becoming an important model. Educators and legislators visited and returned to their home states to promote similar projects. (One year 550 people from eleven states visited the fishery.) Harbuck gave most of the responsibility for interpretation to students, whose talks were replete with scientific detail, personal experience, and pride of ownership. Visitors not only saw a facility; they witnessed consequential outcomes of the work—the informed presentations about and proprietary interests of students in the aquaculture unit.

The project has been successful in part because Harbuck took fully into account where he taught—Florala and water go together. The town surrounds a lake and is only a short drive from the Gulf of Mexico. As might be expected in one of the nation's most water-rich states, streams, ponds, and rivers are close by. The moderate climate, added to the availability of water, makes aquaculture an appropriate enterprise. And this country's annual importation of billions of dollars worth of fish would suggest that it holds good prospects and possibilities for the future of the community and its young people.

The Florala aquaculture unit demonstrates the educational possibilities of place-relevant learning spaces. For me, the first prompt on aquaculture's potential was loaded into a remark by Joe Hankins, a fish biologist and director of the Freshwater Institute of the Conservation Fund, and a consultant for the Florala project. Hankins pointed out that the aquaculture unit was a "living laboratory" rather than the typical "science museum" found in so many schools. There was life in the fish tanks, and he predicted that students' responsibility for and interest in that life would give rise to significant learning. Tears and fish funerals following the early loss of a tank of talapia testified to the youngsters' concern. (I have heard similar stories from teachers involved with other aquaculture programs. Deborah McCord at Loachapoka reports that her elementary students "loved the fish" and wept when they died.) Casual observation reveals that kids are interested in the entire life cycle of the fish, from eggs to harvest. Their increasing ability to operate the systems successfully is evidence of their commitment and their mastery of the tools and processes of commercial aquaculture. The work is important to Florala students, and the responsibility rests essentially on their shoulders—Harbuck estimates that, during school terms, they make 90 percent of the "life and death" decisions. In order to do this well, they have to operate as fish biologists. Their competence has been recognized by employers and by postsecondary institutions interested in recruiting them.

Through their participation in the program, students have mastered the essentials of fish culture. In *Schools for Thought: A Science of Learning in the Classroom,* John Bruer suggests that "learning is the process by which novices become experts."[4] He goes on to observe that "few students can interpret how data support a theory," arguing that without the ability to use data to determine appropriate actions and ask the right questions, it is impossible to move from novice to expert. Bruer suggests further that in order to help students learn, it is essential to provide the "kinds of task environments that will result in the expert behaviors that we want." Harbuck has explained that the lab was a place where he could pursue with the kids the art of asking questions and seeking means to answer them. He did not want his students' eyes dulled by an overload of facts for which they had no use; he wanted them to light up when they "got it." The lab conforms with Bruer's notions of an appropriate "task environment"—it is certainly a place where young people who start with limited science proficiency end up doing the work of scientists.

The connection between gaining competence in the aquaculture unit and learning science was not so quickly grasped in school culture. One science teacher saw the possibilities when his students began explaining pH, a concept whose meaning he had been unable to convey in the classroom. Over time the unit has become a learning context for students who are seeking an advanced diploma and on a college track; college-bound students can be well served by the aquaculture living laboratory. It is important that the school is overcoming educational culture's difficulty in recognizing the benefits of new approaches and its tendency to endorse the artificial division of academic and technical learning and the separation of college-bound and other students.

The problem is illustrated by my conversation with a Florala student whose grades were well below average and of no particular interest to him or, as he suggested, to anyone else. Knowing that he had some responsibility for the fish, I asked him to tell me about his aquaculture work. He immediately catalogued his activities and indicated their rationale: "to keep the fish from going belly-up." He checked and recorded water pH, temperature, and flow; kept an eye on nitrate and nitrite levels; weighed and measured fish. He entered data into computers and reported outcomes. Being thoroughly impressed, I commended him on having learned so much science. He responded quickly that he didn't know much science and that his grades in the subject were always poor. He claimed no effective connection to classroom science although his skills, self-confidence, experience, and interest landed him a job in aquaculture, a field that obviously requires considerable understanding of biology.

Even if nothing else had happened, along with the recognition it received, construction and operation of the aquaculture unit would have satisfied Harbuck. In fact, there was more to come. Successful operation of the facility suggested possibilities for new ways of thinking by administrators, faculty, and students. Hydroponics units were added; specialty fish were raised; a dozen aquariums for the study of genetics were put in place; plans were laid for renting additional aquariums to area professionals and business persons for their offices; a photography lab was added to the complex and a lake was constructed next to it. The project has linked Florala with schools and businesses throughout the United States. It is a model for science instruction, for rural entrepreneurship, for connecting schools to communities and young people to their futures. It illustrates how a locally relevant education program can generate interest within the school and beyond.

I recently saw the potential for the transferring the models developed with Florala teenagers to a program for younger kids at an event combining the dedication of a new greenhouse at Loachapoka Elementary School with the semiannual harvest from its fish pond. The greenhouse is the latest addition to a series of living laboratories that include the fish pond, a nature trail, and gardens. When I entered the greenhouse, I saw fish tanks and a recirculating system that were the same as those used in Florala. The teachers explained that Harbuck had given them a hand. One of his former students, who was attending Auburn University, was guiding them through the development and operation of their hydroponics unit. It was, of course, gratifying to learn that skills and experience were being shared. It was also encouraging to see application of the principles embodied in living laboratories and in all education that is attentive to where students live and the contexts in which they learn.

The observations of participants and the activities of students at the Loachapoka event resembled what I had witnessed elsewhere. The crowd consisted of community members who had built the greenhouse as well as those wanting to buy fish; university representatives who had helped with fish pond management and harvests or who came just to support the venture; the county superintendent of education and board members, who were understandably pleased with their decision to back what is unfortunately an atypical enterprise; and both active and retired school teachers and administrators who had made it possible for their students to participate in such a powerful learning experience. Educators, enthusiastic about the pond and greenhouse, spoke of their connections to important instructional objectives. They were quick to articulate the academic and personal benefits to their students, whose interest was very great. Professionals who supported the project pointed to the potential of living laboratories for engaging kids in scientific work.

The professionals' contentions were borne out by the behavior and conversations of the students. They harvested, measured, sorted, and weighed fish in preparation for selling or transferring them to the new greenhouse tanks. They kept meticulous records and took initiative with little prompting from teachers or resource persons. Displaying a strong sense of ownership, children served as hosts and made clear what they were learning by explaining the operation of the pond and the plans for the greenhouse. They interacted with adults, including a reporter, fish biologists, university staff and other visitors they had not previously met. Their learning environment was rich with life, and it was evident that they had responsibilities for that life—responsibilities requiring considerable understanding of science and mastery of related concepts and techniques.

Loachapoka students had begun with limited scientific knowledge, and yet they had become proficient in important aspects of biology and pond management. Characterized by Deborah McCord, a teacher at the elementary school, as "the biggest learning community I have," the pond has hosted fish, amphibians, insects, and plants, whose scientific names kids are required to know. They learn to use a microscope and to converse with the fish biologists serving as resource persons. All students in the project are expected to do every job and to know the same details about the pond. A number of these children have fared poorly in standard academic settings, yet they have succeeded in the aquaculture work—learning science, taking responsibility for gathering and recording important data about the fish, and dealing with outsiders who come to the site to find out about the program or to buy fish. On one occasion, a visitor asked her third grade guide if she would like to be a scientist. The question elicited a teacher's dream response: "I already am a scientist."

Why do kids learn so much from the living laboratories? For one thing, they love the fish and see the consequences of their actions for the well-being of the pond. They also love having local reporters write about their efforts, having community people visit, and having a chance to work with resource people. Operating in teams where they are accountable to each other, students help raise fish, maintain the pond, and harvest and sell their crops. They are pleased to be called upon to interpret what is happening in the pond and in their learning. And they relish the opportunity to teach others, as reflected in one young student's comment to a group of visitors: "You may not know this, but we have to have bacteria in this pond for our fish to live. I'll tell you why." All this adds up to self-conscious and purposeful learning, growth in self-esteem, and character formation through the fulfillment of real and very public responsibilities and through accountability to peers.

Several outcomes common to the Florala and Loachapoka programs are important affirmations of Consequential Learning approaches. As already pointed out, youngsters with little background in science gain the knowledge and proficiency necessary to operate collaboratively as fish biologists. Although student learning is the primary goal, there are significant ancillary benefits that testify further to the value of Consequential Learning approaches and projects.

Students have fun working in the laboratories. They are dealing with life, aspiring with their peers to shared goals, and seeing immediately the favorable consequences of their actions. My visits to the living laboratories have always confirmed that the kids were happy and enjoying themselves. Harbuck tells the story of a reporter from South Carolina who during her visit to Florala took many photographs of his students in action. She sent Harbuck her published account along with an extensive collection of her pictures and asked: "What is the common thing in all these photos?" Harbuck had no answer, and he was forced to refer to the reporter's observation scribbled on the back of the final image: "They are all smiling." Guided by her perspective, Harbuck then observed for himself that "all you could see were teeth."

The living laboratories at Florala and Loachapoka demonstrate that— given the opportunity and the appropriate information—communities, resource persons and agencies, and funders (including politicians) will back efforts to create and operate relevant learning contexts for students. Both communities have limited financial resources, and their schools have tight budgets—there had been little reason to expect the successful completion of such ambitious projects. Fully outfitted, the facility at Florala cost about $80,000.00; as already noted, it paved the way for other construction. The aquaculture unit was worth much more than the dollar cost given a number of local contributions: grading, leveling, and clearing the construction site; equipment loaned for laying drains and pipes (much of the installation was done by students); fish, feed, chemicals, and other supplies, and the use of nets and brood ponds. The projects not only tapped the latent will of the two communities to contribute to the improvement of their children's education, they demonstrated the power of visionary educators to organize something better for their kids.

Like many teachers directing PACERS projects, Harbuck and McCord say that teachers learn a great deal from this work. For example, watching students in the living laboratories, they discover that kids have previously unobserved interests and abilities. McCord explains that even so-called special education students demonstrate competencies that are unpredictable in routine school settings. And Harbuck reports that he was especially surprised to see particular youngsters assume strong leadership roles for the first time. Their observations indicate that, given appropriate opportunities, kids who are considered poor or indifferent students often show that it is not their ability or motivation that is wanting but the prevailing modes of instruction and evaluation.

I have noticed that Harbuck, McCord, and other teachers working in similar settings, tend to talk like biologists. That is scarcely surprising since professional scientists have become their colleagues, helping them to carry out challenging science-based tasks. As a result, the teachers are introduced to new concepts and new ways of thinking, an outcome they prize. And research shows that it is valuable for students—especially minority and rural students—to learn science from scientists and to establish collegial relationships with them and with other adults in order to make science relevant and beneficial to their communities.

One of the most important developments relating to the living laboratories was initiated by Florala students who were not themselves participating in the aquaculture work. On hearing a rumor that the program was to be closed, they circulated a petition calling for its continuation; the response from other students indicated a school-wide appreciation of the fish-farming venture. Whether the closure was in the offing or whether the petition changed any plans is not the issue. What is important is the unprompted and collaborative action of students, through which they affirmed ownership and assessed the instructional potential of a school program. They knew it was making a difference, and they believed they could as well.

Section 4

Consequential Learning Issues

The programs and approaches gathered under the Consequential Learning heading have implications for education policy and practice and are also impacted by them. Consequential Learning may suggest paths for reform, build on existing processes, or clash with the status quo. Calling for education that values the citizenship and membership of young people in communities, with the resulting connection of learning to place, it does not necessarily reflect prevailing systemic educational values. It is concerned with increased local governance, lively contexts for learning, equity, the relationship of schooling to young people's futures, the cultivation of civic virtue, entrepreneurship, and self-determination. Those inclined to use similar approaches and to undertake similar projects will, therefore, have to consider these related matters. The following essays offer reflections on what I judge to be serious issues surrounding any effort at education reform that follows the approaches and embraces the values advocated by Consequential Learning.

The Value of Place

Content and process, what and how—these are main categories around which education theorists gather. Given the impact on the lives of students of the places where they live, "where" has become my category of choice. The selection does not diminish the importance either of subject matter or pedagogical theory and practice; it does argue for taking very seriously the places in which schools exist and the contexts in which young people live, learn, and prepare for their futures. Paying attention to place can give direction to practice and relevance to content.[1] Although the congregation in the "where" category is growing, it is not yet the case that current educational practice is strongly influenced by considerations of place.

My own ruminations on place and education became focused in the early 1970s, when awareness of the wisdom of using solar power in a sun-favored state like Alabama was growing. At that time I was working with several people and groups engaged in passive solar construction—south facing construction. Their projects amazed me: cost effective solar homes, food dryers, water heaters, and greenhouses. As a result I added a passive solar greenhouse to the south side of my barn—with the glazing angled to catch the winter sun at its lowest point. It was a great place to be in cold weather or when it was filled with seedlings for the garden. I enjoyed it until a tornado deposited a significant portion of a large pine tree directly on the structure. That loss prompted many conversations on greenhouses. In one airport exchange, a man told me that he too had built a greenhouse which was intended to serve as a context for teaching his kids about plants and gardening. They were enthusiastic about his idea and about the building itself, so much so that the man felt it necessary to insist that the children could not enter the greenhouse without him. In due time, he found one of them, his five year old daughter, alone in the greenhouse. Before he could apply parental sanction, she pointed at him and declared, with considerable cheek, "Everybody has to be somewhere."

The significance of her point is consistently explored in literature, even though it remains essentially unrecognized by educators. In *Mr. Jefferson's Lost Cause*, Roger Kennedy quotes Albert Cowdrey's observation that southern writers "know in their bones" that "there is no life apart from place, and no place is exactly like any other." Kennedy pursues the theme through Eudora Welty's contention that her writing, and that of other southern writers, is "bound up in place." I would add Charles Frazier's concern for knowledge of place, as expressed in *Cold Mountain* where his two central female characters, Ada and Ruby, are polar opposites with respect to this knowledge. Frazier says of Ruby, "She seemed to delight in demonstrating how disoriented Ada was in the world." Plants, animals, seasons, directions, and sources of water were mysteries to Ada who was educated but not "placed."

I would argue that rather than being particularly southern, the awareness of place that Kennedy describes is widespread. He could easily have cited Willa Cather or Wallace Stegner or any number of nonsouthern writers. As is reflected in a great deal of literature, all people are from somewhere, they live somewhere, and their identities, knowledge, perceptions, and ways of knowing are shaped by specific places.

Placeless education forfeits all the potential arising from connection to locale, including relevance and motivation. Why is connection to place not pivotal in educational practice? The standardization of curriculum and teacher preparation and assessment has, of course, been instrumental in removing consideration of place from the learning process. But there are other factors. One lies in the general direction of modern society. In *The Fate of Place: A Philosophical History,* Edward Casey notes that "the idea of place . . . is . . . deeply dormant in modern Western thinking."[2] Casey's assertion came to mind while I was reading Gerald Grant and Christine Murray's *Teaching in America: The Slow Revolution* which demonstrates the power of teacher-posed questions to motivate students in ways that lead to exemplary work.[3] One question they cited asked students how they would describe their school to a young person who was soon to transfer there; the second invited seventh graders to consider whether their town's streams were becoming more polluted. Unlike many classroom questions, these related to the students' world and, therefore, to what they knew and cared about. They required more than simply giving back to the teacher previously deposited information; they called upon students to observe, acquire knowledge, and make judgments on their own. With respect to the status of local streams, Grant and Murray report that the kids collected and analyzed water samples and presented their findings to the town board. The authors' contention that good questions can provoke good learning is well-documented, but the dominant power of place to promote interest and action remains in this case unexamined.

Consequential Learning advocates that it is essential for people to know where they are in the world, and, therefore, that public education connect learning with place. In *Ecological Literacy,* David Orr argues for a new canon of required reading that would result in knowledge of place—of latitudes and longitudes, watersheds and ecological communities, geological as well as human history, weather patterns, and indigenous grasses and trees.[4] He rightly concludes that ignorance of such matters is pervasive and the consequences have important negative environmental implications. Similarly, teachers planning

PACERS projects often talked about the need for kids to gain local environmental knowledge—especially knowledge of where their water originated and how to measure and ensure its quality. Like Orr, they wanted students to understand, protect, and enjoy the environments in which they lived. To achieve their goals, however, teachers had to create or identify new contexts for study and to write materials relevant to their local situations. Underpinning their often ambitious goals was a commitment to preparing young people to be citizens and to take responsibility for the well-being of their communities, including the ecological communities.

The planning of PACERS teachers was based on a knowledge both of where their students lived and of their students' concern for those places. Two incidents have stuck with me as special reinforcements of my appreciation of teachers' understanding and have helped keep me focused on the significance of place for young people. One involved an SCCH interview for summer health fair positions. Two first-year students at the University of Alabama, who came from a rural community that had hosted an SCCH health fair, were interviewing together at the tail end of the staff selection period. They were questioned about why they had waited so late to apply given that they knew first-hand about the fairs through their own town's partnership with the SCCH. They answered that their time on campus had been limited because they had been going home frequently to stay with a young widow and help care for her children. Impressed by their response, one of the interviewers remarked that it was good to hear that they were doing community service. The students were befuddled by the comment, and after a pause they said, almost in unison, that they were not doing service in their community, that they lived there. In terms I have used throughout this book, they held membership. Although community service and the related notion of service learning are important, they are not as fundamental as membership—a reality that implies responsibility as an ordinary part of life rather than as an extraordinary service.

The second incident involved a PACERS project in which high schoolers in Akron, Alabama were adding passive solar greenhouses to the homes of seniors with limited incomes. The greenhouses reduced utility costs and provided new gardening opportunities for several of the community's elderly members. At the time, the PACERS Cooperative was struggling to get on its feet and was seeking funding from a major national foundation that had agreed to send a program officer to conduct a one-day site visit. It was crucial to use the time well, since so much rested on the outcome. PRSR staff decided that the program officer should begin by visiting an Akron greenhouse and talking with the students who had built it. No other adults were to be in the greenhouse; PRSR staff and their teacher were to stand outside, leaving the matter in kids' hands. The foundation officer, surrounded by rural youngsters from a state he had never visited, broke the inevitable ice by asking about the angle of the glazing on the greenhouse. It was the right question, and it generated a flood of specific science and math-based answers, beginning with a recitation of the formula for obtaining the most light at the winter solstice at Akron's latitude and moving to an explanation of the use of water-filled barrels on the back wall to take advantage of water's ability to absorb heat quickly and release it slowly, thus moderating greenhouse temperature. And so the conversation proceeded with young people explaining to an interested adult strategies for passive construction, materials that are required, and purposes that can be served by a greenhouse.[5]

During the conversation, the homeowner emerged to greet

the kids and their visitors. She thanked the students and their teacher again for what they had done, and explained to the foundation's program officer and the PRSR staff that it meant a great deal to have the greenhouse and to know the youngsters. It was an instructive moment in regard to what students can do to make a difference in their communities. It became even more instructive when the students said that seeing the greenhouse made them proud of what they had done; they were sure it would be a marker to which they would return for years to come.

Place was the key: The specificity of latitude and angles of the sun shaped the design of the greenhouse. The opportunity to contribute to their community motivated the students to do good work. They became adept at learning and applying tools and concepts of science, math, and construction by building greenhouses that were additions to their own community and that stood as a testimony of their ability and concern.

I have not found it difficult to be an advocate for emphasizing "where" in education. I have had the great privilege of watching young people develop and demonstrate mastery of significant information, concepts, and skills when their learning is related to place and when it evokes their natural desire to make a difference in their communities—to exercise the rights and obligations of citizenship and membership.

Rural Schools: Resources for Community Development

As we hammered away on the 2 x 6 decking for a playground platform, one of the volunteers began telling me the painful details of the closing of his school. Rightly confident of a sympathetic audience, he recounted with practiced precision the details and outcomes of the closure. The litany was the common one: the town had lost its heart; people moved away; kids dropped out of school; it was hard to feel or take ownership for a new and distant school; participation in extracurricular activities had become difficult for students, parents, and community. The man's emotional recounting of the consequences made me listen even though there was nothing new until his closing sentence: "It was forty years ago, but I feel it like it was yesterday."

His forty-year memory of the death underscored the perceived value of rural schools to communities and their members which includes, but goes beyond, the teaching of numbers and letters. It is my experience that small rural schools teach the basics well despite shamefully low funding and the debilitating presence of poverty in many Alabama towns. As dominant local institutions, however, they serve more comprehensive roles. Keepers of memories and identities, rural schools fulfill a significant and prized function in these days of "bowling alone." Through the inevitable class photographs that line hallways, they archive the generations of their graduates. Many alumni return to have a look; reunions call back other grads, even some cast far across the country in America's rural diaspora. These schools also support a community identity; local memory and tradition are tied to them. Considerable good will or perhaps "social capital" accrues to rural schools because of their connection to individual and corporate identities.

The accomplishments of rural schools are a singular source of pride; their events set calendars. These schools are common ground; sometimes they are the only place where communitywide aspirations are formed and realized. Small communities also understand that their economic well-being is tied closely to their schools because they have a concentration of professionals, a stable payroll, and access to information and technology. Their students are capable and have strong interests in contributing to their communities. Schools are often the most significant local institutions in rural America. It may not be too much to say that their continuation is for many small communities a confirmation of their own existence.

For more than a century maintaining an identity and a viable existence has been difficult for rural communities. Loss has been their lot. Their populations have declined, and their ablest members have often moved to urban areas to earn their livings and apply their talents. Family farmers have lost their farms or work under heavy mortgages as powerful and policy-favored industrial agriculture has become dominant. No institution has been more important to rural communities than the family farm. Its failure has brought rural life into serious jeopardy and foreshadowed other closures. Locally owned businesses, banks, post offices and doctors' offices, as well as schools have routinely followed.

The sources for the revitalization of rural America are not clear. Industrialization is unlikely to be the main long-term solution. There are indicators that recreation and leisure interests could yield considerably more outcomes than service jobs, especially if entrepreneurial skills are cultivated. It is conceivable that the agricultural models of the Amish or small scale specialty and low-input farms might take hold. Adding value locally to raw materials can increase benefits from the traditional extractive enterprises. Whatever emerges, schools must play an important role in sustaining and rebuilding rural communities. The vision of schools must be expanded; their functions must exceed what can be pursued through standardized curricula or measured on standardized tests. Building upon community trust and good will and upon their strengths as key local institutions, schools are in a unique position to be engaged in community development.

To illustrate their potential role, I will cite three areas of work that can be mutually beneficial for schools and communities. Rural schools can create appropriate models for improving local life; they can develop entrepreneurial skills and attitudes; and they can gather and distribute pertinent information. These are not the only means by which the schools can contribute to community development, but they are significant and, as reflected in Consequential Learning programs, their pursuit will also improve students' learning and opportunities.

Although it is by no means a systemic principle, the notion that schools can add directly to local community development through the introduction of appropriate models shows up at times throughout the rural United States. In *Foxfire Reconsidered*, John L. Puckett describes the work of Andrew Ritchie, an educator from Rabun County, Georgia. Ritchie returned to his Georgia mountain home from Harvard with a degree and the idea that a school can be an instrument in improving local life.[6] In 1905, he founded Rabun Gap Industrial School to give tangible expression to that theory which reached its fullest expression with the institution's addition of its Family Farm Program. This program, a model for improved agriculture, established more than thirty farms as demonstration sites for tenant farmers. I note Ritchie's efforts because they were large scale and helped create room for an expanded vision of schools' capacity. I cite them also because they were not generic and related directly to the needs, interests, and economics of specific rural communities. In my own work in the PACERS Cooperative, I have already referred to schools that have undertaken successful community related initiatives that developed aquaculture units, solar construction, and technology programs. They have provided local farmers with prototypes for improved agriculture, promoted low cost energy efficient shelter design, and have changed the technology infrastructure of entire counties and the on-line educational opportunities for all students in the state.

Rural schools have a history, however episodic, of creating models that simultaneously enhance community well-being and make learning relevant. Unfortunately, the benefits have not led to any significant change in the guiding vision of what rural schools can and should be. The development of locally appropriate models is not reflected in curriculum and budgets and is not articulated in pre-service and in-service professional development of educators. The potential is not being tapped or systemically reflected.

Jonathan Sher pushed the notion that rural schools must prepare their young people to create jobs in their communities, in his words "to make a job, not just take a job." That notion led to the formation of REAL Enterprises, a national organization dedicated to helping schools realize Sher's purpose. Its efforts have had community-enhancing consequences throughout rural America. Other educators, organizations, and schools, including community colleges, have likewise seized upon the need to promote entrepreneurial "literacy" and opportunity in rural areas. The American rhetoric of a participatory economy based on individual initiative would seem to make entrepreneurship an indispensable part of education. It is not. As pointed out by REAL and other education organizations, students' entrepreneurial confidence and interest fall off dramatically as they pass through school. The decline, predictable in a passive educational culture, is troubling for a participatory economy; it is devastating for rural areas. Made passive in part by dominating external industrial, urban, and cultural models, rural communities desperately need to take initiative in shaping their futures. I have said for many years that rural county commissioners have stiff necks from watching the skies for the descent of saving factories. They do not fall very often, and they have a tendency to fly away early. I do not gainsay factories' value and there are powerful examples of industries having a pivotal impact on communities. I am nonetheless convinced that local initiative is indispensable and that schools must foster such initiative and help create the dispositions, skills, and opportunities that will make it viable. Programs, curriculum, evidence, and models are available and eagerly promoted. The challenge is for schools and communities to create and support visions of education that value initiative and entrepreneurship.

Good information is essential for making good decisions. In rural communities, there is often a deficit of accurate information; schools can locate, create, and distribute such information in a timely fashion. I have seen students in rural Alabama help design and conduct useful economic and health inventories, publish community newspapers, retrieve and analyze census data, test and record water quality, write local histories, and keep information on families, churches, and other local institutions. In the process, they have demonstrated their capacity and eagerness to use databases and statistical software and to gather and interpret facts on which individuals and communities can act. Their work has provided a context for community reflection on issues as important as gas pipeline locations, land use, and taxation. Outcomes have included new and expanded businesses, support for local tax increases, and changes in the plans of a major utility corporation in order to insure the safety of the local elementary school. Similar student efforts in rural communities elsewhere in the United States have provided local businesses with information they needed to survive and have boosted local commerce and revenue through sophisticated analysis of the results of out-of-county/community spending.

The United States has changed from an industrial to an

information economy, and students who gather, create, publish, and act on information will be prepared to enter that economy. In the process, they can provide their communities with indispensable data and broaden the notions of the purposes for schools that are now basically recipients of externally generated and selected information that they are mandated to transmit to their students. They are judged on their capacity to promote student retention of that information. For rural communities and simply for good education, schools must also be institutions that value and foster the creation, analysis, evaluation and distribution of information—skills that are indispensable for citizenship and for participation in an open and democratic economy.

Given their capacities, community-based public schools can be a valuable resource for reconstructing rural America (and I think deteriorating neighborhoods). The closing of schools has been disastrous; however, the failure to understand and act upon the potential of those remaining would be unthinkable. In order to build upon and control their resources, communities in rural America need appropriate and indigenous models for enhancing community and individual well-being, obtaining timely information, and infusing entrepreneurial initiative and skill. Schools can contribute all of these and more. In partnership with their communities, schools can be agents of change. If they are, their students will have a better education, their communities may have better prospects, and schools will begin to fulfill even more their potential as central institutions in rural America. There are many individuals, and organizations, and communities that would knock nails into that kind of education platform. They might even be able to tell stories of how communities and schools worked together to become sustainable and healthy.

All They Want to Do Is _____

What do young people want to do? With manifest disappointment, some educators in small rural Alabama schools have said: "All they want to do is work in the mill." Their response reflects a strongly held view by teachers, counselors, and principals that their students, whom they know very well, can do better than work in the "mill" or take low-paying jobs that represent the path of least resistance. It also reveals frustration with some young people for their failure to appreciate the relevance of school for their futures. It is grounded in the belief of educators that those they teach have more talent than options.

Several years ago, when a teacher in a small rural school in the Pine Belt of southwestern Alabama told me that all one of her students wanted to do was work at the *New York Times*, she added a very different perspective. The student had helped establish and later edited the school-based and student-published local community newspaper. The competencies, confidence, and associations developed through this work had engendered an aspiration that was fulfilled some years later when he was offered an internship at the *Times*. In interviews leading to establishing the paper, I had asked him why he was interested. Revealing a powerful motivation, his first answer was: "I want to give my community a voice." He made it clear that membership in his own community mattered. His comment, not unlike that of many other young people, represented a variation on the theme "all they want to do is work for their communities."

I have been associated with many small rural schools (15-75 per grade) in Alabama, primarily through the PACERS Cooperative. The schools are diverse. Some are located in the Black Belt and are almost entirely African-American; some are Appalachian and until the immigration of Latinos, had limited minority enrollments. Most of the schools are integrated, some with black and others with white majorities. They are grossly under funded even by the standards of Alabama—a state that invests less in students than almost any other. Poverty is so predictably characteristic of the schools that a principal once told me his school's 40 percent free and reduced lunch rate was low. In such situations, young people have difficulty accessing a variety of good options. Yet every school with which I have been connected has exemplary graduates whose stories are quickly recounted and whose achievements are a source of pride. They have been successful in professions and occupations beyond the "mill" and beyond their communities and state, generally in urban settings. Significantly, these exemplars have often been joined by a number of their peers in exercising postsecondary-school options.

In documenting choices of graduates of several economically disadvantaged Appalachian and Black Belt schools, I found that students routinely wanted more than to take the path of least resistance. Many enrolled in post-secondary education institutions, some entered the military, and some went directly to urban-based employment. The outcomes were strongly influenced by school size. As the growing body of research indicates, the strengths of small schools contributed to better results than circumstances would have been predicted.

I have seen the benefits of small schools. In them, students are known and personally encouraged, are participants and contributors—all factors that help keep them in school and to graduate. Not surprisingly the word chosen most often by teachers and students to describe their schools is family. Sometimes symbolized by no locks on the lockers, violence, vandalism, and behavioral problems are less pervasive than in schools with more students. There are few cracks through which youngsters can fall; school staff are positioned to know and care about students' life choices. It has become clear through research and practice that young people in poverty, as well as most other students, do better in small schools. As a result they have greater chances of enjoying better futures. It is, therefore, particularly unfortunate that schools are getting larger. Rural School and Community Trust publications note that the average number of students per school in the United States was 127 in 1940. By 2002, it had grown to 653. In sticking with outmoded industrial models of schools, and by chasing elusive bottom lines, education policy makers persistently dismiss the benefits of small schools in favor of factory-sized complexes. The trend must be reversed if schooling is to be improved.

The small schools with which I have been privileged to be associated are good places. Their students aspire to do better and take advantage of opportunities to do so. They want more options and connections. It was no surprise to me to hear about the youngster who only wanted to be on the staff of the *New York Times*. Through partnerships in demanding projects in more than fifty schools, I observed rural students and interacted with them. Many consistently demonstrated competence, aspiration, and commitment; and they eagerly took hold of new challenges they were provided through a variety of projects. Along with many of their teachers, they worked hard and effectively. Kids who had previously been seen as without schoolhouse smarts were able to exploit their own abilities and interests and to experience success. Motivated in part by a desire to improve their communities, these students published local newspapers, built low-cost energy efficient houses and passive solar greenhouses and computers and computer networks, wrote local histories and assessed local water quality, documented the lives of elders through music and drama, established businesses, completed health and community surveys, and introduced the Internet to their "beyond the digital divide" communities.

Students, representing the spectrum of school enrollments, gained competence and self-awareness; and they made connections necessary to pursue careers that were not accessible to them prior to their participation in the projects. In the course of that experience, students effectively applied concepts and tools of technical, academic, and artistic disciplines to produce public outcomes of local benefit. They did the work of scientists, historians, builders, and publishers; and they did so, in part, through association with resource persons who supported their work, confirmed their capacities, and helped them make connections that would figure in their futures. The production of publicly valued outcomes and the association with professionals also helped create a self-awareness through which students could begin to achieve a sense of self-determination necessary to act upon new opportunities.

I know that rural students, including those who live in poverty, want more than low-paying jobs. I know that they are competent to exercise significant postsecondary-school options. I know that small schools help young people who will seize opportunities to improve their prospects. But kids need their schools to expose them to even more worthwhile possibilities. In short, the program and process of education have to change. For starters and as examples, it would be helpful if schools were connected to and routinely engaged external resources (e.g. professionals, agencies, employers) and if schools and students kept data likely to be more useful than the results of standardized tests—tests that are invariably loaded against the children of poverty.

The projects cited above were carried out in schools that

opened their doors in order to gain the needed support of persons who were not their employees. Those projects required expertise, experience, and connections unavailable in the schools. It was fairly easy to persuade agencies, postsecondary institutions, local volunteers, and professionals to participate by creating contexts and tasks that called upon them to share their vocational skills and interests and that involved them directly with students to accomplish significant tasks. Obviously there were some impediments. Standardized curricula and standardized tests conform schools and threaten to turn them into franchises. They foster standardized thinking and standardized modes of operation that tend to keep the doors shut, not only to outside expertise and experience, but also to new ideas. Participating in the projects, I observed that often administrators had difficulty understanding that the work could be correlated to state education requirements and that it would increase student interest and achievement.

Not only are schools too removed from their constituencies, the use of their time and energies are dictated by standardized tests. Their hearts are set on "testing well." They do so because tests are the only measure of student achievement and the only form of evaluation that the media, education policy makers, and politicians care about. As a result, schools that serve young people in poverty are forced to bear an additional burden. Poverty does not prepare kids for success on standardized tests. Test results do not reveal fully the abilities of poor kids; they are more likely to confirm their most dominant variable, the income of their families. So schools in poverty, already denied the standard resources to support equity in standardized tests, must devote disproportionate time and energy to the development of test-taking skills. As one teacher explained to me: "our school is frozen from January through the tests in April." Her point was clear, all classroom work was focused on improving examsmanship, while the normal routines were abandoned. In some cases, extracurricular activities were dropped in pursuit of test results that would remove sanctions against schools; another version of the old military judgment that the town was to be saved by its destruction. I would be more sanguine about the tests if they were preceded by an influx of funds and resources and if they were balanced by other measures.

Standardized tests do not reveal enough. To paraphrase Walker Percy, you can be in the "99th percentile and flunk life." Or you can be failed by tests that do not tell the whole story of your competence, confidence, interest, and circumstance. Other data are needed to help young people assess their own skills and reach better futures and to render schools better able to assist them with both.

Students should keep evidence of the outcomes of their learning and work. In the dominant context of external evaluation, creating and reflecting on personal portfolios seem indispensable. Good practice in portfolio assessment has been documented, and the rationale is supported by research.[7] The push for developing metacognitive skills in students increases the need for personal portfolios, for the retention and examination by students of their representative work. Awareness of oneself as a learner is indispensable for success in education and in life. It can be promoted through portfolio creation and assessment easily integrated into the kinds of projects advocated in Consequential Learning.

If teachers and administrators believe that students can do better and that they should see the relevance of education for their futures, then it seems logical that schools should make themselves accountable in those terms. How do schools record the options taken by their students? How much is known of the "whats" and "whys" of student choices? How do administrators and faculties develop curricular and extracurricular activities that open options to students, that give evidence of an intention to help young people make their way to successful futures? What agencies and individuals can invest productively in the schools and how can they be recruited to do so? These are important questions that should be persistently addressed by schools if they want for their students more than the path of least resistance. Clearly educators, with the help of outside resource persons, must do much more to link their young people to their futures than arrange a sprinkling of college and career days.

Rural students I have known are capable. They will make good vocational decisions based on experience and opportunity. However, for many rural youngsters who are already circumscribed by poverty, schools must become more engaged in the informed and comprehensive promotion of a wider array of options. They must recruit external allies and develop connections. They must help their young people assess their own capacities, and they must understand what happens to their graduates. After all, students will most likely opt for what they know about and believe they can do.

Who Owns Schools Anyway?

It was already hot, Alabama summer hot. The "gymnatorium" was overflowing with parents, siblings, grandparents, and other kin and friends gathered for kindergarten graduation. The principal explained to the perspiring witnesses that he had tried all day to have the "air" turned on. The controls, however, were in the school system offices in the county seat—twenty miles away. Climate control is always an issue during late May in Alabama; in a gym filled with hundreds of taxpayers concerned about their be-robed young scholars, it was the issue. Sweating with the other grandparents, I asked myself what seemed a reasonable question: "Who owns schools anyway?"

Neither an unbearably hot gym nor the question were new to me. Thirty years of work in partnership with small rural schools and communities across Alabama had repeatedly raised the issue of ownership. Unrelenting school closures and consolidations during that time had made clear that small rural Alabama communities, like many towns and neighborhoods throughout the United States, do not own their schools. It is possible to gloss over this judgment by reference to the right to vote or to address school boards and school professionals. In reality in Alabama's countywide systems, those rural communities that are not county seats are almost always without significant political power, and certainly have no influence over the state board and department of education. State mandates, like those eventuating in large comprehensive high schools, resulted in closed schools and punishingly long bus rides. With the best and worst intentions, county boards, the local agents of governance, routinely have reverted to school consolidation as the only means considered for survival or improvement. Across decades, decision makers at state and county levels have followed the industrial model of education and have persisted in the belief that bigger is better and more cost-effective. The most ardent of education reform groups have considered the issues of school size, the distance of schools from students and families, community ownership, and devastating bus rides to be relatively inconsequential.

Research and perspectives that challenged school closure were not effectively admissible in school board deliberations. Issues of concern to rural communities—school size, drop out rates, the negative effect of distance on student achievement and participation as well as on family and community involvement—were not up for serious discussion. Ironically, the technology of the fossil fuel burning bus was preferred to the emerging digital-based capacities that could move information rather than people and that could help move the state forward technologically. As I had learned from educators and school supporters in other states, school closures following the same patterns and resulting from the same rationale, were not limited either to Alabama or to rural areas.

Local communities were bereft of standing and often ill-prepared to deal with threatened school closures. They were not ready because, even in the face of overwhelming evidence, it was inconceivable to community members that their schools could be closed. When aroused to act to keep "their" schools, they were frequently regarded as selfish and uncommitted to the welfare of the county—an ironic judgment in a time of reduced public support for public schools. Other small communities in the same counties, trying to hold onto their own prospects, were more likely to loosen the rope than to make common cause with those whose schools were already on the guillotine. The perspectives of communities seeking to retain their schools were routinely dismissed. They were not "owners," they lacked proprietary claim on the schools, and they were not cordially invited to the table of public discourse. The emotional exchanges between community members and boards were substitutes for deliberation between relative equals; they produced heat but no light. I have seen only a handful of decisions to keep schools open and none of those is beyond reversal.

The closures were massive and inevitable. As already noted, the principal ammunition for closure was the persistent and increasingly dubious belief that bigger is better and more cost-effective. The gun was an educational system that left many communities voiceless and without ownership. In the twentieth century, school closures throughout the United States were preceded by consolidation of thousands of school districts and an increase in state power over schools. Paradoxically for a democratic educational system, there were growing numbers of students, parents, and taxpayers in America while the number of school boards and citizen decision makers declined. Educational governance became more centralized and concomitantly more professionalized. Authority moved away from communities as students rolled out of town on busses headed for schools located many miles away. The "ownership" of schools became less and less local. To many communities and their members, fee simple felt distant and professional, and nonpublic began to define the education of their children.

During the crises surrounding school closures, communities demonstrated strong if episodic commitment. Community members tried to organize and act together, but they were ill prepared. Before facing the prospect of losing their schools, few communities displayed interest in organizing local education foundations or other associations that might support and even challenge their schools. There were virtually no "Community School Organizations" to complement the more narrowly defined parent and teacher associations. The crisis of closure revealed that local communities usually lack the experience, expertise, and motivation to organize for the purpose of deliberating with, supporting, evaluating, and challenging their schools and school systems over the long term. The absence of local authority, and consequently the practice of ownership, contributed to the general inability of communities to express their aspirations for the education of their young people and for their schools.

Matters relating to educational hopes and values are generally left to centralized authority, professional educators, and elite state or national support and reform groups. Whatever good they may do, I do not think their results can replace the benefits to be derived from the contributions and sustained proprietary interest of local citizens and organizations—the publics closest at hand.

I support public education even though I increasingly choose to speak of it as tax-supported rather than public. I affirm that existing state and local public school boards and public education professionals have done many things right. I know they often operate in contexts where public schools are asked to address, with inadequate resources, some of society's most intractable problems. I endorse the need for statewide standards (though not as the sole measure) and for federal efforts to secure equality. I even suppose that the centrally controlled thermostat has saved money and insured equitable distribution (or nondistribution) of cool air to schools in my county. But, as a taxpaying grandparent sitting in my puddle of sweat and thinking about closed schools, diminishing community authority, the terrible drop-out rate in American schools matched by the astonishing growth of home schooling, and the growing distance between the public and public schools, I could swear I heard: "Pay the power bill, but keep your hands off the thermostat."

By Numbers Alone? By What Numbers Then?

Every person and every institution are to be held accountable—well, maybe not every person and every organization but certainly every public school. Public schools are the poster children for a world of being held accountable, and I am troubled by the rhetoric of school accountability. In part because it is completely tied up in numbers, with the only admissible ones being those ginned up by standardized testing. Having worked in grossly under resourced schools, I wonder why the accountability statistics do not include the number of books in the library; the number of up-to-date working computers, the numbers showing the health and wealth status of students (the "wealth numbers"—rather than their schools or teachers—are, of course the singular index of how kids will test out), the numbers that specify and allow comparison of the resources available to schools and school systems, and the numbers that reveal whether state and federal governments are supporting the testing push (or the latest and likely unfunded mandate) and providing needy schools with resources to help them avoid being substandard. Of course, these numbers bear on the accountability of the public and of policy makers to kids and schools, and, at present, the spotlight is only on schools.

Accountability, based only on test scores, should be suspect in the complex world of teaching and learning. In *School Testing: What Parents and Educators Need to Know*, Estelle Gellman observes: "Tests do provide useful information, but they also have their limitations, limitations that must be considered when test scores are used in educational decision making. A test score doesn't necessarily tell the truth about an individual; we should neither blindly put our faith in test scores nor discard them ... Instead we should use them judiciously and put them in their proper place in the evaluation process."[8] Currently test scores constitute the only element, and, alone, they are oversimplified and media-friendly but incomplete keys to understanding how to realize a better future for public schools.[9]

It should be noted also that the word "accountability" is first cousin to "accounting." From Enron forward, accounting practices have demonstrated the potential for digital deception. Numbers can hide the truth, and they can be made to serve the purposes of those who own the books. (We were warned long ago by Mark Twain that numbers are useful, if not always straightforward, instruments for prevarication.) In terms of school accountability, numbers are made to lie when they are regarded as simple and complete indicators of whether public schools and their employees are doing right by the taxpayers. Test scores do not tell the whole story, and by themselves they are not the whole truth. I do not question the need for testing and strong standards, but would rather not sit on the stool of school accountability until a couple of more legs are added.

My experience, in many significantly under funded but productive rural schools, has also prompted me to question the capacity of the prevailing test score rhetoric to illuminate the accomplishments, goals, needs, and shortcomings of public education. From my perspective, "accountability" seems to be more like a bullet aimed at public schools than like a commitment of public support. The call for accountability appears to be premised on the widespread and frequently unchallenged assumption that public schools are failing badly and increasingly dangerous. It seems to be taken for granted that schools, and especially teachers, are not accountable and that they will not be so unless there is a bit in their mouths and the hand of the highest authority pulling on the reins.

Is the assumption of failure based on fact or is it a perception that might even be fostered by ideological and/or uninformed perspectives? Are the problems faced by some schools basically ones transferred to them by society itself? For example is the presence of violence in schools (albeit it seems to be declining) unexpected in a society willing endlessly to commend mayhem to youngsters? The present time is one in which anti-public rhetoric is well-funded, seemingly media institutionalized, and politically correct—it may willingly foster a wrong or incomplete judgment about public education. In the fifty years since I graduated from high school in Alabama, good things have happened in or because of public schools: state literacy rates have improved; African-American students throughout the state now have access to school busses; a greater percentage of the increasing numbers of high school graduates are attending postsecondary academic institutions; kindergarten is now available. The graduation standards are stricter and a more demanding curriculum is in place, and it appears that the great increase in requirements goes unnoticed. In this regard, most observers of public education, therefore, might be surprised by Deborah Meier's observation: "Schools are asked to achieve an extraordinary goal—to provide all children with the kind of schooling once offered to a small elite."[10]

Beyond academics, Alabama public schools have made some significant, if incomplete, efforts to abide by court orders to integrate and to ensure racial equity. I have seen and worked with schools and school systems trying to determine how to serve Latino young people whose immigration has been swift and has had less backing by organizations than earlier civil rights efforts. Schools have been required to deal with the challenges of pluralistic society—including equity. They have done so more effectively than churches and probably better than other nongovernmental institutions in the state. Yet Alabama's schools, and I suspect those in other states, are still reeling from their attempts to address the problematic legacies and realities of segregation. They are given little credit for what they have done, and they have been abandoned by many precisely because of their efforts to be inclusive and equitable.

The accomplishments of public schools and the realities with which they must deal, including the mandate to educate all children, seem to have little effect on the perceptions by which they are judged. Several examples illustrate my point. In a conversation with a well-educated businesswoman from another state, I was explaining technology business projects undertaken through PACERS in Alabama's Cherokee and Hale counties. The projects, which have been noted above, required students to develop and apply complex digital and business management skills and to interpret their work to politicians, school board members, and business people—including the head of a major national corporation. As the scope and requirements of the projects became clear, she commented ruefully "It's too bad that can't be done by public schools and their students." When I assured her that the projects had, in fact, been carried out by youngsters in public schools, she immediately changed the subject. Her point had not been, as I initially assumed, that she wanted these options for public schools; she simply dismissed those institutions as incapable of such demanding work. My accounts were shelved in the fiction stacks.

This woman's judgment was echoed by one of the candidates for the presidency of the United States in the 2000 campaign. Seated in the midst of private school students, he was discussing with them a character-building program in which they were participating. He had high praise for them and the program, and noted to the camera that you could find no such initiative in a public school. I was shocked that he felt free to pass such a blanket judgment on public education, and I knew from my own experience that the opinion was unfounded. Upon hearing his comment, I thought immediately of a gathering of rural elementary school teachers who had come together to share ideas and experiences relating to the PACERS Book Shows project. The teachers had been provided with Caldecott and Newbery Medal-winning books and other exemplary children's literature for use in their classes; in return they were expected to help students make public presentations on the books, both to promote interest in reading and to show parents and others what the kids were learning. The teachers' conversation included extensive observations on how to use the books to help meet the state's directive to provide instruction related to character formation. My point is twofold. What supposedly could not be found in public schools had in fact been mandated in Alabama, as in other states. More important the teachers were devoted to their students' moral development and cited cogent examples of how the appropriate use of good books had fostered character-related discussions. It is worth noting that the schools in the Book Shows project merited more public support than they got; these institutions were expected to fulfill public mandates and to serve a very diverse and needy student population that deserved more help than they would ever receive. Expecting teachers to make bricks without enough straw is, I suppose, no less appropriate than assuming that public schools have no interest in the moral formation of their students.

Both the businesswoman and the candidate had reached sweeping but incorrect conclusions about public schools. I do not know the route they had taken to reach their assumptions. Perhaps they had seen some bad schools or bad teachers. There are of course frequent examples of both; but there are also plenty of bad businessmen and bad corporations; some bad doctors and bad health care organizations. Why don't people assume the worst about business which persistently calls for more trust and less regulation, or about the health care industry, with its increasing and perhaps even inequitable charges to its consumers? Whatever the reason, many hold the opinion that public education is guilty of the grossest incompetence, that it has uniquely fallen short of the accountability standard, and that the road to quality is paved with test scores. I do not think that public education has failed—although some schools, administrators, and teachers have. I know that very strong reform and assistance is needed, but I do not believe that higher test scores will result in more tax support and greater public respect. After all many of the current numbers do not justify the dismissive labels routinely hung on public schools.

In the introduction to *Making the Grade*, Tony Wagner examines the pervasive notion that American public schools are failing—overwhelmingly. He contends that Scholastic Aptitude Test (SAT) scores and the National Assessment of Education Progress (NAEP) suggest progress over the last three decades. "More students are taking advanced courses in high school, and the number of students who graduate and attend college continues to rise . . ."[11] If the public schools are such failures, Wagner ponders, how has the nation been able to enjoy such great prosperity in the extremely competitive worldwide economy of the past decade or so. Wagner advocates for fundamental education reform; he does not deny that there are some miserable schools and school systems. He is appropriately arguing for reform based on a clearer understanding of the status of public education and what is necessary to make it fully relevant. His view underscores my own conviction that numbers cannot by themselves change public perceptions or, for that matter, reform education.

Well, what can make a difference? As argued throughout this book, greater local ownership of and involvement in schools are crucial to improved education and for more accurate assessment of outcomes. It is often noted that most people think that their local school is better than schools in general. Although this judgment may not reflect reality, it does make clear that the closer people are to schools, the more likely they are to value them. Proximity can make a difference, and it can provide multiple points of assessment to which schools and teachers are entitled and from which new perspectives may be gained and contributions made. I have been fortunate to be able to observe and work with a number of Alabama schools that do not test well, but that have enjoyed significant accomplishments. My experience in one of them helps explain my take on the issue of accountability, and my conviction that public student-produced outcomes helps "outsiders" evaluate schools from new perspectives and with tangible data.

Monroe Senior High School (MSHS) is located near the Alabama river in Monroe County, Alabama. Separated by the river from the county seat, it has also been separated from resources to which its students are entitled. In this respect it is not unlike many schools in the poorest of Alabama's rural counties. Nearly all its students are African-American, and nearly all are eligible for free or reduced-priced lunches. Before becoming associated with the PACERS Cooperative, MSHS had few current books in its extremely limited library. The school for several years has been under fire because of its students' low test scores—closure and state takeover have been persistent rumors fueling the virtually exclusive preoccupation with preparing students to be better test takers. Given the power of testing to dictate the actions of administrators and teachers, there seemed to be nothing else to do but to improve examsmanship.

A variety of initiatives with the school, gave me multiple perspectives on its students—perspectives that told a different story. Through the Awards Program in Writing, referenced earlier, all the youngsters in two grades wrote essays and poems that were collected and published. Although the quality varied, all students demonstrated the ability to write, and together they produced work that was humorous, revealing of local life, and indicative of their concern for school, family, friends, and community. The county newspaper published complimentary articles about the work of the students—work that was tangible, public, and subject to direct evaluation even by professional writers.

With support from the Monroe County school system, the PRSR and the PACERS Cooperative initiated and evaluated an interactive, computer-based instructional program as a means to offer MSHS students, for the first time, foreign language courses. The program involved two other schools, and, therefore, the teacher was able to compare the performance of MSHS students with others in the county. They did well; in fact, they did so well that MSHS was chosen as the primary site at which the PRSR and PACERS would test the potential of on-line instruction for use in rural schools. Before the courses could be offered, however, the school had to be wired and servers had to be installed. Students helped in wiring the school; and they learned how to help maintain and operate the servers, and they interpreted what they were doing to visitors interested in learning about networking and on-line instruction.

The Virtual High School in Cambridge, Massachusetts provided the initial curriculum that would be available to students at MSHS and at other sites around the country. The courses were demanding—so much so that after discussing them with MSHS students, the superintendent of education in Alabama observed that the courses were more like college work than high school fare. It was assumed that economically poor students in a school with limited science instruction would not be competitive. They were competitive. Their grades were high, and the students were also able to explain both what they were learning and how this new mode of instruction functioned. Given the opportunity, students demonstrated ability, interest, and commitment; and the school principal and staff challenged and assisted them. The success and observations of MSHS students figured prominently in PRSR and PACERS planning that led to the creation the Alabama On-line High School (AOHS). With backing from the Alabama State Department of Education and other agencies, the AOHS now offers a variety of courses required for high school graduation and provides instructional opportunities otherwise unavailable to many Alabama students. It is a powerful resource for achieving equity across the state, and it owes a great deal to kids who tested poorly but performed well.

My perspective on MSHS students has been formed primarily through collaborative initiatives that demonstrated their ability to learn, to accept responsibility, and to be competitive in a challenging academic environment when they had the proper support. This kind of information may not tell the whole story, but it tells more about the kids at MSHS than can be learned simply by test scores. These youngsters always made it clear that if the public were accountable to them, they would be accountable in return.

My experience over time in many schools like MSHS has not suggested that they are all they could be, or that all their teachers and administrators are working as well as they could, or that reform is not needed. Nonetheless, their accomplishments have been greater than the support they have received, and suggest that to judge public schools only by their students' test scores is misleading. It covers over the reality that the improvement sought will come only when the public itself decides to be accountable to all children, and the public is more likely to make that decision when it can see and be involved directly in the life of schools.

Conclusion

HOW PUBLIC IS PUBLIC EDUCATION?

Several years ago David Mathews raised the question: Is there a public for public education? *In Schools We Trust,* Deborah Meier presents approaches to and examples of schooling intended to help restore public trust in public education. After a long and difficult political battle to direct more of an Alabama county's tax money to public schools, a member of a board on which I served announced: "to hell with the public." In his political sphere, he—not unlike others past and present—thought that the only chance of saving public education was to by-pass the public. All three rightly suggest that public support for public education is in question and that effective connections between the public and schools are not the order of the day. The lack of such relationships is particularly costly at a time of declining American trust in almost all things public.

Whether the loss of public trust is warranted is debatable, however, the reality is not. In order to build a stronger public for public education and to improve schools, it is necessary to be clear on causes for the disconnect and fashion trustworthy remedies. A likely beginning place for the identification of the reasons for the great divide and the remedies to bridge it may begin with another question: "How public is public education?" The question presupposes that it may not be public enough—either for those on the inside or those on the outside. That is to say that the loss of trust may correlate with the failure of educators, policy makers, and taxpayers to pay sufficient attention to "public" as the modifier of education—the primary word by which educational content, practice, and evaluation should be determined. Ironically, it seems more accurate to speak of education as professional or bureaucratic or even political (implying that it is the concern more of politicians more than of the populace) than to speak of it as public. Public denotes the source of revenue for schools, and the fact that, unlike private schools, they must serve all children.

I do not think that public education is public enough for the student citizens on the inside or the tax-paying citizens on the outside. The internal and external shortfalls are connected and in some cases the problems for those "outside"—people who are not political decision makers, school board members, education professionals, or members of powerful organizations positioned to demand attention from policy makers—and for those on the "inside"—students—stand together. The basic factors that diminish the public nature of education for the outsiders have been examined above, and in summary fashion are restated here.

The governance of schools, including goal setting, is not widely distributed and is too remote from communities. Governance has moved from communities, to larger systems (e.g. county-wide), to state, and more powerfully than ever to the federal level in the No Child Left Behind legislation. The move to a federally controlled education system changes, perhaps reverses, the former roles held at local, state, and federal levels, and positions Washington to set the standards, evaluate the results, and hand out the punishments for failure, if not the funds for remedy. Continually growing in average size, schools and school systems are already too large to encourage and support the participation of parents, to say nothing of the public in general. The evaluation of schools is increasingly professionalized and centralized; the complex meanings of the numbers generated in the process are not directly accessible to the public. There are few options for the public to see the actual work of students. (I often think that school architecture and security systems reflect the diminishing chances for the public to see what kids do in school. Fences, security check points, and smaller windows all fit a pattern suggesting that the public is not welcome and that the shades have been drawn. Perhaps school administrators do not trust the public either.) Curriculum is standardized; it does not significantly include place or comprehensively address diversity, and its implementation does not often reflect an appreciation for an array of learning styles. Outsiders with expertise and interest have few entry points into schools. And it now appears politically correct to bash public schools, and the bashing seems to be media institutionalized—a condition that cannot be remedied by the present devotion to testing numbers which, in their surface simplicity, seem to tell the whole story, and, thereby, remove most incentive for in depth examination of issues.

These factors and others come into play in relationship to the "insiders" as well. Students are citizens and members of places, however, it does not appear that the curriculum and culture of public education take seriously these and, in fact, other basic student identifiers. For example in our society a growing percentage of young people are obese and physically inactive. It would appear as a result that schools might offer more physical and health education opportunities to kids. Maybe some do, but in my experience these subjects are low priority. In a comparable way, with the society's declining participation in the political process, it seems more necessary than ever for the promotion and recognition of citizenship to become core values in schools. If it were, public education would become more public for those on the inside for the following reasons.

School size would be reduced. Researchers tracking the impact of school size have for about fifty years proved that the smaller the school the greater the participation by all students—of course participation includes academics. Small schools draw in minority and poor students, and, thereby, extend hospitality to those most likely to be left out. The larger the school the greater the likelihood of producing spectators. Smaller schools are contexts that are more likely to engage participants—a result to be highly valued by a democratic society in terms of its politics and economics.

Entrepreneurship and active learning would be firmly included in educational practice in order to cultivate young peoples' capacity to define the course of their own lives. Following the same line, schools would be more and more places where kids were producers not consumers. Students would be challenged to use tools, concepts, and information to create products that could make a difference to their communities, and they would be expected to have knowledge of the places where they live. The process of public production develops skills for use in the public arena. Students would be assisted in the art of self-evaluation, and come to value their inherent right to determine their own competence. In schools young people would consistently come to know adults, "outsiders"—many of whom would be experts sharing skills and experiences that are direct links to kids' futures. Recognizing that collaboration in the production of beneficial outcomes is an important element in character formation and civic life, schools would provide opportunities for young people to work together to identify, achieve, and evaluate common goals.

As a starting point for addressing these issues, I have proposed Consequential Learning, an educational approach for making schools more public (inside and out) through principles and formats that value students' citizenship and membership and that challenge youngsters to do work that has transparent consequences for them and for the places where they live. I am convinced through experience that such work creates a new proximity for direct public evaluation of schools and helps them to become more fully public institutions. Building upon students' inherent ethical interest in making a difference, Consequential Learning creates means for public engagement in schools—an engagement that brings crucial experience and resources into schools, that creates skills and personal and institutional connections important for students' futures, that connects schools to their communities, and that prepares a foundation for public-driven systemic reform.

NOTES

Notes to the Introduction

1. Amy Gutmann, *Democratic Education* (Princeton: Princeton University Press, 1999), 3.
2. I have been fortunate to work with rural educators and education organizations throughout the United States, as well as in Australia, Canada, New Zealand, and Norway. They have helped shape the ideas in this book and confirm that the concerns addressed in it are common in current education practice.
3. Tony Wagner, *Making the Grade* (New York: Routledge Falmer, 2002), 10.
4. For example see Thomas Toch's *High Schools on a Human Scale*. Toch's research, sponsored by the Gates Foundation, confirms and updates small school benefits including lower dropout rates and reduced teacher turnover.

Notes to Section 2

1. The Community Services Project was a multi-year program in which university students contracted with rural communities to undertake local improvement projects. Generally projects were summer long, related to students' majors and career interests, and provided services or resulted in the development of local facilities including parks and clinics.
2. Deborah Meier, *In Schools We Trust* (Boston: Beacon Press), 10.
3. David Mathews, *Why Public Schools? Whose Public Schools? What Early Communities Have to Tell Us* (Montgomery: NewSouth Books, 2002), 64.

4. John D. Bransford, Ann L. Brown, and Rodney R. Cocking, editors, *How People Learn: Brain, Mind, Experience, and School,* expanded edition (Washington D.C.: National Academy Press, 2000), 245-247.
5. Robert Putnam, *Bowling Alone* (New York: Simon and Shuster), 304.

Notes to Section 3

1. Although the PCNP has been almost exclusively a rural project, it has had an urban expression in city schools with predominantly African-American populations. The responses of students in urban schools were similar to those of rural youngsters. African-American students expressed the need to supplement the reporting on their communities by local dailies and to be sure that more was being covered than "death and destruction."
2. A good example of student media is cited and supported by the Education Foundation's Kids Can Do Program (http://www.educationfoundation.org.au). The Melbourne, Australia based foundation's Autumn 2003 Kids Can Do newsletter provides information on SYN (Student Youth Network) 90.7. In EF sponsored conversations with several Melbourne young people involved in the operation of a school-based radio station, I was struck by the connections between their interests and objectives and those of students in rural Alabama schools. Although obviously Melbourne is a media rich city, the young people with whom I talked understood themselves to be providing a unique service to and perspective on young people and clearly understood that their complex media work was preparing them for the future and that it was a unique and strongly motivating circumstance for learning.
3. AlabamaREAL has provided assistance to many PCNP newspapers by helping them develop business plans and strengthen the entrepreneurial aspects of their programs.
4. John Breur, *Schools for Thought: A Science of Learning in the Classroom* (Cambridge: MIT Press, 1993), 13.

Notes to Section 4

1. In this essay the focus is upon the positive impact of place upon student learning, however attention to place can create new roles and form important associations for schools. It is important to emphasize that Consequential Learning is about expanding schools goals and connections and in developing their capacity to serve their communities.
2. Edward S. Casey, *The Fate of Place: A Philosophical History* (Berkeley and Los Angeles: University of California Press, 1984), xi.

3. Gerald Grant and Christine E. Murray, *Teaching in America: The Slow Revolution* (Cambridge: Harvard University Press, 1999), 39.
4. David Orr, *Ecological Literacy* (Albany: State University of New York Press, 1992).
5. I have encountered the assumption that education connected to place means that students' learning is restricted to local matters and does not prepare them for life in a mobile society. The greenhouse conversation shows that student interest in local made math and science applicable and accessible anywhere.
6. John L. Puckett, *Foxfire Reconsidered: A Twenty Year Experiment in Progressive Education* (Urbana and Chicago: University of Illinois Press, 1989).
7. In the Spring of 2004 the state of Nebraska persuaded the federal government to allow the use of portfolio assessment as the means of testing and assessment. The state's education commissioner, Douglas Christensen said that "education was too complex to be reduced to a single score. If it's bad for kids, we're not going to do it" (*Alabama School Journal*, April 12, 2004).
8. Estelle Gellman, *School Testing: What Parents and Educators Need to Know* (Westport: Praeger, 1995), 165-66.
9. For example, Anne C. Lewis, with reference to Southeast Center for Teaching Quality at Georgia State University (*Education Digest*; Feb2004, Vol. 69), reports that teachers in six southeastern states support standards-based reform and state accountability systems, however, they found few connections to needed or implied professional development and in lower-performing schools "teachers felt threatened and under the gun to use 'drill and kill' kinds of instruction."
10. Deborah Meier, *In Schools We Trust* (Boston: Beacon Press, 2002), 2-3.
11. Tony Wagner, *Making the Grade* (New York: RoutledgeFalmer, 2002), 3

Bibliography

Benjamin Barber, *Strong Democracy: Participatory Politics for a New Age*. Berkeley: University of California Press, 1984.

John D. Bransford, Ann L. Brown, and Rodney R. Cocking, editors, *How People Learn: Brain, Mind, Experience, and School*, expanded edition. Washington D.C.: National Academy Press, 2000.

John T. Bruer, *Schools for Thought: A Science of Learning in the Classroom*. Cambridge, Mass: MIT Press, 1993.

Edward S Casey, *The Fate of Place: A Philosophical History*. Berkeley: University of California Press, 1998.

Winifred Gallagher, *The Power of Place: How Our Surroundings Shape Our Thoughts, Emotions, and Actions*. New York: HarperCollins, 1994.

Estelle Gellman, *School Testing: What Parents and Educators Need to Know*. Westport: Praeger, 1995.

Gerald Grant and Christine E. Murray, *Teaching in America: The Slow Revolution*. Cambridge, Mass: Harvard University Press, 1999.

Amy Gutman, *Democratic Education*. Princeton: Princeton University Press, 1987 and 1999.

Tony Hiss, *The Experience of Place*. New York: Random House, 1991.

Alfie Kohn, *The Schools Our Children Deserve*. New York: Houghton, Mifflin, 1999.

David Mathews, *Why Public Schools? Whose Public Schools?* Montgomery: NewSouth Books, 2003.

David Orr, *Ecological Literacy*. Albany: State University of New York Press, 1992.

John L. Puckett, *Foxfire Reconsidered: A Twenty-Year Experiment in Progressive Education*. Urbana and Chicago: University of Illinois Press, 1989.

Robert Putnam, *Bowling Alone*. New York: Simon and Schuster, 2000.

Diane Ravitch, *The Schools We Deserve: Reflections on the Educational Crisis of Our Time*. New York: Basic Books, 1985.

Diane Ravitch, *The Troubled Crusade*. New York: Basic Books, 1983.

Tony Wagner, *Making the Grade: Reinventing America's Schools*. New York: Routledge Falmer, 2002.

WAKE TECHNICAL COMMUNITY COLLEGE LIBRARY
9101 FAYETTEVILLE ROAD
RALEIGH, NORTH CAROLINA

DATE DUE

GAYLORD   PRINTED IN U.S.A.

NOV '05